THE ULTIMATE CRICKET TRIVIA QUIZ BOOK

A Collection of 370+ Trivia Quizzes
for Cricket Lovers

MARK DEVIS

Copyright © 2024 by Mark Devis

All rights reserved. No part of this publication may be reproduced, distributed, or transmitted in any form or by any means, including photocopying, recording, or other electronic or mechanical methods, without the prior written permission of the publisher, except in the case of brief quotations embodied in critical reviews and certain other noncommercial uses permitted by copyright law.

TABLE OF CONTENTS

Introduction 1
Chapter 1: The Origins of Cricket 2
   Quiz Answers 7
   Did You Know? 9
Chapter 2: Legendary English Cricketers 11
   Quiz Answers 16
   Did You Know? 18
Chapter 3: Iconic Cricket Grounds in the UK 20
   Quiz Answers 25
   Did You Know? 26
Chapter 4: The Ashes - A Historic Rivalry 28
   Quiz Answers 33
   Did You Know? 35
Chapter 5: Great Cricket Rivalries 37
   Quiz Answers 42
   Did You Know? 45
Chapter 6: World Cup Wonders 47
   Quiz Answers 52
   Did You Know? 54
Chapter 7: Memorable Matches 56
   Quiz Answers 61
   Did You Know? 63

Chapter 8: Innovations in Cricket (T20, The Hundred) 65
   Quiz Answers 70
   Did You Know? 71

Chapter 9: The Evolution of Cricket Equipment 73
   Quiz Answers 78
   Did You Know? 80

Chapter 10: Controversies and Scandals 82
   Quiz Answers 87
   Did You Know? 90

Chapter 11: The Role of The ECB 92
   Quiz Answers 97
   Did You Know? 99

Chapter 12: Women in Cricket 101
   Quiz Answers 106
   Did You Know? 108

Chapter 13: Cricket Coaching and Development 110
   Quiz Answers 115
   Did You Know? 117

Chapter 14: Cricket in Pop Culture 119
   Quiz Answers 124
   Did You Know? 126

Chapter 15: Future of Cricket in the UK 128
   Quiz Answers 133
   Did You Know? 135

Conclusion 137

INTRODUCTION

Welcome to a captivating journey through the world of cricket! This book is designed for enthusiasts who cherish the history, nuances, and vibrant culture of this beloved sport. Whether you're a seasoned fan or new to the game, our collection of quizzes, and astonishing "Did You Know?" facts offers a unique exploration of cricket's rich legacy and its evolution.

In each chapter, we dive deep into various themes, from legendary players and historic matches to cricket's integration into pop culture and its exciting future in the UK. Our quizzes challenge your knowledge and provide a fun way to engage with the material, while the answers section helps solidify your understanding of intricate details and lesser-known trivia.

The "Did You Know?" segments are crafted to astonish and enlighten even the most knowledgeable fans, revealing hidden gems and intriguing insights about cricket's impact both on and off the field. These facts are not just informative but are designed to spark curiosity and conversations among readers of all ages.

This book serves as both a testament to cricket's enduring appeal and a tool for fostering a deeper appreciation of its complexities. It is perfect for personal enjoyment, quiz nights, or as a gift to the cricket aficionado in your life. Prepare to be entertained, educated, and inspired as you flip through the pages of this comprehensive guide to one of the world's most cherished sports.

So, grab your bat, don your cap, and step onto the pitch as we explore the extraordinary world of cricket through quizzes, answers, and fascinating facts that illuminate every corner of the cricketing universe. Let's play!

CHAPTER 1:
THE ORIGINS OF CRICKET

1. What year is considered as the earliest definite reference to cricket being played?

    a. 1598
    b. 1611
    c. 1533
    d. 1654

2. Where was cricket believed to have been originated?

    a. India
    b. England
    c. Australia
    d. South Africa

3. Which English monarch is famously associated with an early mention of cricket?

    a. King Henry VIII
    b. Queen Elizabeth I
    c. King Charles I
    d. Queen Victoria

4. What was the primary material used to make the earliest cricket balls?

    a. Wood
    b. Leather stuffed with feathers
    c. Solid rubber
    d. Cloth

5. In which century did cricket become a major sport in England?

    a. 16th century
    b. 17th century
    c. 18th century
    d. 19th century

6. The earliest known game of cricket was played in which county?

    a. Kent
    b. Surrey
    c. Sussex
    d. Essex

7. Which one of the following laws was formally codified first?

    a. LBW (Leg Before Wicket)
    b. No ball
    c. Wide ball
    d. Bouncer

8. Who is known as the Father of Cricket?

    a. WG Grace
    b. Donald Bradman
    c. William Gilbert Grace
    d. Tom Richardson

9. In which year was the first known set of written cricket rules created?

    a. 1744
    b. 1700
    c. 1774
    d. 1699

10. The first recorded match of "great cricket" was held between which teams?

    a. Hampshire vs Kent
    b. Sussex vs Surrey
    c. Kent vs Surrey
    d. London vs Guildford

11. What significant change in cricket equipment occurred in the 18th century?
    a. Introduction of the cricket bat handle
    b. Use of leather cricket balls
    c. Wearing of protective gear
    d. Development of spiked shoes

12. Which country outside England first formed a cricket club?
    a. India
    b. Australia
    c. United States
    d. South Africa

13. In what year did the legendary Hambledon Club form, contributing significantly to cricket's development?
    a. 1750
    b. 1764
    c. 1780
    d. 1776

14. What was unique about the cricket bats in the 17th century compared to today's bats?
    a. They were made of metal
    b. They were shaped like hockey sticks
    c. They had no grip
    d. They were two-sided

15. The oldest cricket competition still played today was first contested in which year?
    a. 1825
    b. 1709
    c. 1864
    d. 1780

16. What is the Artillery Ground famous for in the history of cricket?
    a. It hosted the first international cricket match

    b. It was the site of the first recorded century by a batsman
    c. It was a notable venue for major matches in the 18th century
    d. It was where the first cricket club was founded

17. Who was the first player to write a book about cricket?

    a. John Nyren
    b. Sir Len Hutton
    c. Sir Don Bradman
    d. W.G. Grace

18. The MCC, which later became the standard-bearer for cricket laws, was founded in which year?

    a. 1787
    b. 1751
    c. 1800
    d. 1726

19. What significant role did Thomas Lord play in cricket history?

    a. He invented the cricket ball
    b. He founded Lord's Cricket Ground
    c. He was the first professional cricket coach
    d. He designed the first cricket uniform

20. In which year was the first international cricket match played?

    a. 1844
    b. 1877
    c. 1900
    d. 1930

21. Which two teams played in the first official Test match?

    a. England vs Australia
    b. England vs India
    c. Australia vs South Africa
    d. England vs South Africa

22. When were overarm bowling techniques first legalized in cricket?

a. 1864
   b. 1901
   c. 1825
   d. 1845

23. Which famous cricket club, founded in 1787, is known for its pivotal role in the development of modern cricket rules?

    a. Marylebone Cricket Club (MCC)
    b. Hambledon Club
    c. Surrey County Cricket Club
    d. Yorkshire County Cricket Club

24. The first known women's cricket match was played in which year?

    a. 1745
    b. 1844
    c. 1902
    d. 1932

25. What type of wood is traditionally used to make cricket bats?

    a. Oak
    b. Willow
    c. Pine
    d. Maple

Quiz Answers

1. **A – 1598.** The year 1598 is considered the earliest definite reference to cricket being played. This reference was found in a court case concerning ownership of a plot of common land in Guildford, Surrey.
2. **B – England.** Cricket is believed to have originated in England. Historical references suggest the game was played in southeastern England as early as the medieval period.
3. **B – Queen Elizabeth I.** Queen Elizabeth I is famously associated with an early mention of cricket, as it was known to have been played during her reign in the late 16th century.
4. **B – Leather stuffed with feathers.** The earliest cricket balls were made of leather and were stuffed with feathers. This type of ball was used until the development of modern cricket balls with a cork core.
5. **C – 18th century.** Cricket became a major sport in England during the 18th century, with the formalization of rules and establishment of cricket clubs.
6. **C – Sussex.** The earliest known game of cricket was played in Sussex. This region is often credited with being one of the birthplaces of modern cricket.
7. **B – No ball.** The "no ball" law was one of the earliest cricket laws to be formally codified, helping to standardize how deliveries were bowled.
8. **C – William Gilbert Grace.** William Gilbert Grace, commonly known as W.G. Grace, is known as the Father of Cricket. He was an influential figure in the development of the sport during the 19th century.
9. **A – 1744.** The first known set of written cricket rules was created in 1744. These rules were formalized by the London Cricket Club.
10. **C – Kent vs Surrey.** The first recorded match of "great cricket" was held between Kent and Surrey. This match took place in the early 18th century and marks one of the earliest instances of inter-county competition.

11. **A – Introduction of the cricket bat handle.** In the 18th century, the significant change in cricket equipment was the introduction of the cricket bat handle, which helped players better manage the heavier and harder leather balls being used at the time.
12. **C – United States.** The United States was one of the first countries outside England to form a cricket club, with clubs established as early as the 18th century.
13. **A – 1750.** The Hambledon Club, which played a major role in the development of cricket, was formed around the year 1750 in Hambledon, Hampshire, England. This club is often regarded as the cradle of cricket.
14. **B – Shaped like hockey sticks.** Cricket bats in the 17th century were unique because they were shaped like hockey sticks. This design was conducive to hitting a ball that was rolled along the ground, as was the style of play at the time.
15. **B – 1709.** The oldest cricket competition still played today, the County Championship, was first contested in the year 1709. It began with matches between various county teams in England.
16. **C – Notable venue for major matches in the 18th century.** The Artillery Ground in London is famous in the history of cricket for being a notable venue for major matches during the 18th century, particularly involving the London Cricket Club.
17. **A – John Nyren.** John Nyren was the first player to write a book about cricket. His work, "The Cricketers of My Time," provides insights into the players and the game during the late 18th and early 19th centuries.
18. **A – 1787.** The Marylebone Cricket Club (MCC), which later became the standard-bearer for cricket laws, was founded in the year 1787. The MCC has been a pivotal institution in the development and regulation of cricket.
19. **B – Founded Lord's Cricket Ground.** Thomas Lord is significant in cricket history for founding Lord's Cricket Ground in London, which is often referred to as the "Home of Cricket" and remains a central venue for international cricket.
20. **A – 1844.** The first international cricket match was played in the year 1844. This historic match was between the United States and Canada and took place in New York.

21. **A – England vs Australia.** The first official Test match was played between England and Australia in 1877. This match, held in Melbourne, marked the beginning of Test cricket.
22. **A – 1864.** Overarm bowling techniques were first legalized in cricket in the year 1864. This was a significant evolution from the underarm bowling that was prevalent during cricket's early years.
23. **A – Marylebone Cricket Club (MCC).** Marylebone Cricket Club (MCC) was founded in 1787 and has played a crucial role in the history of cricket. It is renowned for being the custodian of the Laws of Cricket, having rewritten them in 1788 to bring order and structure to the game. The club's influence on the development of cricket is profound, with its headquarters at Lord's Cricket Ground in London, often referred to as the "Home of Cricket.
24. **A – 1745.** The first known women's cricket match was played in the year 1745. This match took place in Surrey, England, and represents an early example of women participating in the sport.
25. **B – Willow.** The type of wood traditionally used to make cricket bats is willow. Specifically, cricket bats are usually made from a type of willow called "cricket bat willow," which is prized for its toughness and shock-resistance.

Did You Know?

1. Cricket is one of the oldest team sports still played today. The first recorded cricket match took place in Kent, England, in 1646.
2. King Charles II was an avid cricket fan, and his patronage helped elevate the status of the sport during the 17th century.
3. In the 18th century, cricket became a major gambling sport in England. Noblemen would sponsor matches and bet large sums on the outcomes, significantly increasing its popularity.
4. Early cricket bats looked much like hockey sticks, curving outward at the bottom. It wasn't until the 1770s that the straight bat was introduced, which made it easier to play the length ball.

5. The first recorded women's cricket match was played in 1745 in Surrey, England, challenging the notion that cricket was exclusively a man's sport from its earliest days.
6. The world's first international cricket match was played between the USA and Canada in 1844 at the St George's Cricket Club in New York.
7. Early cricket balls were made of wool and covered with leather. They were notoriously hard to see, leading to many injuries.
8. Cricket was spread across the world by the British military and colonists. It quickly took hold in the British colonies, particularly in Australia, India, and the West Indies.
9. Often referred to as the "Cradle of Cricket," the Hambledon Club in Hampshire, England, was one of the first cricket clubs established in the 1760s and played a major role in developing the modern game.
10. Founded in 1787, MCC was initially a social club for gentlemen cricketers but soon took on the responsibility for drafting and updating the laws of cricket.
11. The world's first dedicated cricket ground was the Artillery Ground in London, which became the home of cricket from 1730 to 1770.
12. Cricket is mentioned in the works of great writers like Jane Austen and Charles Dickens, highlighting its cultural significance in England during the 18th and 19th centuries.
13. It wasn't until the late 19th century that protective equipment like pads and gloves became commonly used. Before that, batsmen played without any protective gear.
14. The term "laws" rather than "rules" is traditionally used in cricket, emphasizing the game's historical and cultural importance.

CHAPTER 2:
LEGENDARY ENGLISH CRICKETERS

1. Who is known as the "Father of English Cricket"?
    a. Ian Botham
    b. Geoffrey Boycott
    c. W.G. Grace
    d. Jack Hobbs

2. Which English cricketer was famously called "The Master"?
    a. Len Hutton
    b. Jack Hobbs
    c. Alastair Cook
    d. Joe Root

3. Who was the first English cricketer to reach 10,000 runs in Tests?
    a. Graham Gooch
    b. Alastair Cook
    c. Alec Stewart
    d. David Gower

4. Which English bowler is known for "The Ball of the Century" in the 1993 Ashes series?
    a. James Anderson
    b. Stuart Broad
    c. Shane Warne
    d. Ian Botham

5. Who captained the England team to their first-ever Cricket World Cup win in 2019?

a. Joe Root
   b. Eoin Morgan
   c. Ben Stokes
   d. Jos Buttler

6. Which English cricketer is the leading wicket-taker in Ashes history?
   a. Stuart Broad
   b. Ian Botham
   c. James Anderson
   d. Fred Trueman

7. Who was the first cricketer to score a triple century for England?
   a. Wally Hammond
   b. Andrew Strauss
   c. Len Hutton
   d. Alastair Cook

8. Who set the record for the highest individual score in a single Test innings for England with 364 runs?
   a. Len Hutton
   b. W.G. Grace
   c. Alastair Cook
   d. Kevin Pietersen

9. Which English cricketer was known for his controversial "walking" in the 2008 series against New Zealand?
   a. Michael Vaughan
   b. Andrew Flintoff
   c. Kevin Pietersen
   d. Paul Collingwood

10. Who was the youngest player to captain the England cricket team?
    a. Ian Botham
    b. Michael Atherton
    c. Joe Root
    d. Alastair Cook

11. Which cricketer won the BBC Sports Personality of the Year in 2005 after the Ashes victory?

    a. Andrew Flintoff
    b. Kevin Pietersen
    c. Michael Vaughan
    d. Steve Harmison

12. Who is the highest run-scorer in a single day of Test cricket for England, scoring 309 runs?

    a. Ian Botham
    b. W.G. Grace
    c. Len Hutton
    d. Alastair Cook

13. Which English bowler famously took 19 wickets in a Test match against Australia in 1956?

    a. Jim Laker
    b. Stuart Broad
    c. James Anderson
    d. Fred Trueman

14. Who was the first English cricketer to be knighted while still playing?

    a. Ian Botham
    b. Jack Hobbs
    c. W.G. Grace
    d. Alec Stewart

15. Which English player was known for his "never-say-die" attitude and all-round cricketing skills?

    a. Ian Botham
    b. Geoffrey Boycott
    c. David Gower
    d. Freddie Flintoff

16. Who was the first Englishman to take 100 wickets in One Day Internationals?

a. Darren Gough
b. Stuart Broad
c. Ian Botham
d. James Anderson

17. Which player scored the fastest Test century by an English cricketer?

    a. Ben Stokes
    b. Ian Botham
    c. Jonny Bairstow
    d. Jos Buttler

18. Who is the most capped English Test cricketer?

    a. James Anderson
    b. Alastair Cook
    c. Ian Botham
    d. Alec Stewart

19. Which cricketer has the most centuries for England in Test cricket?

    a. Alastair Cook
    b. Kevin Pietersen
    c. Joe Root
    d. Geoffrey Boycott

20. Who was the English cricketer famously involved in the "Bodyline" series?

    a. Douglas Jardine
    b. Harold Larwood
    c. Wally Hammond
    d. Bob Willis

21. Which cricketer holds the record for most runs in a calendar year for England?

    a. Michael Vaughan
    b. Joe Root
    c. Alastair Cook
    d. Kevin Pietersen

22. Who led England to their first T20 World Cup win in 2010?
    a. Paul Collingwood
    b. Eoin Morgan
    c. Stuart Broad
    d. Andrew Flintoff

23. Which English batsman was renowned for his defensive technique and high number of not outs?
    a. Geoff Boycott
    b. Chris Tavare
    c. Alastair Cook
    d. Joe Root

24. Who is the only English cricketer to have taken 400 Test wickets and scored over 5,000 Test runs?
    a. Ian Botham
    b. Stuart Broad
    c. James Anderson
    d. Freddie Flintoff

25. Who among the following was England's captain during the infamous "Stanford Super Series"?
    a. Andrew Strauss
    b. Kevin Pietersen
    c. Ian Bell
    d. Paul Collingwood

Quiz Answers

1. **C – W.G. Grace.** W.G. Grace is known as the "Father of English Cricket" due to his dominant influence and significant contributions to the sport during his career.
2. **B – Jack Hobbs.** Jack Hobbs, famously called "The Master," was renowned for his skillful batting and prolific run-scoring during the early 20th century.
3. **B – Alastair Cook.** Alastair Cook was the first English cricketer to reach 10,000 runs in Tests, achieving this milestone in May 2016 against Sri Lanka.
4. **C – Shane Warne.** Although Australian, Shane Warne is known for "The Ball of the Century" in the 1993 Ashes series, a leg-spin delivery that bowled Mike Gatting.
5. **B – Eoin Morgan.** Eoin Morgan captained the England team to their first-ever Cricket World Cup win in 2019, leading them to victory over New Zealand.
6. **C – James Anderson.** James Anderson is the leading wicket-taker in Ashes history among English cricketers, known for his skill as a swing bowler.
7. **A – Wally Hammond.** Wally Hammond was the first cricketer to score a triple century for England, achieving this feat against New Zealand in 1933.
8. **A – Len Hutton.** Len Hutton set the record for the highest individual score in a single Test innings for England with 364 runs against Australia in 1938.
9. **A – Michael Vaughan.** Michael Vaughan was known for his controversial "walking" decision in the 2008 series against New Zealand, choosing to walk despite not being given out.
10. **D – Alastair Cook.** Alastair Cook was the youngest player to captain the England cricket team, taking on the role at the age of 25.
11. **A – Andrew Flintoff.** Andrew Flintoff won the BBC Sports Personality of the Year in 2005 after playing a key role in England's Ashes victory.

12. **C – Len Hutton.** Len Hutton holds the record for scoring the most runs in a single day of Test cricket for England, amassing 309 runs against Australia in 1938.
13. **A – Jim Laker.** Jim Laker famously took 19 wickets in a Test match against Australia in 1956, setting a record for the most wickets in a single Test.
14. **C – W.G. Grace.** W.G. Grace was the first English cricketer to be knighted while still playing, recognized for his profound impact on the sport.
15. **D – Freddie Flintoff.** Freddie Flintoff, known for his "never-say-die" attitude, was an influential all-rounder with remarkable skills in both batting and bowling.
16. **A – Darren Gough.** Darren Gough was the first Englishman to take 100 wickets in One Day Internationals, achieving this milestone in 2001.
17. **C – Jonny Bairstow.** Jonny Bairstow scored the fastest Test century by an English cricketer, reaching the mark in just 46 balls against New Zealand in 2022.
18. **B – Alastair Cook.** Alastair Cook is the most capped English Test cricketer, having played 161 Test matches.
19. **A – Alastair Cook.** Alastair Cook has the most centuries for England in Test cricket, with a total of 33 centuries.
20. **A – Douglas Jardine.** Douglas Jardine was the English cricketer famously involved in the "Bodyline" series as the captain who employed the controversial bowling tactic.
21. **B – Joe Root.** Joe Root holds the record for most runs in a calendar year for England, having scored 1,477 runs in 2021.
22. **A – Paul Collingwood.** Paul Collingwood led England to their first T20 World Cup win in 2010, captaining the team in the tournament held in the West Indies.
23. **A – Geoff Boycott.** Geoff Boycott was renowned for his defensive technique and high number of not outs, known for his cautious and meticulous approach at the crease.
24. **A – Ian Botham.** Ian Botham is the only English cricketer to have taken 400 Test wickets and scored over 5,000 Test runs, showcasing his exceptional all-round skills.

25. **B - Kevin Pietersen.** Kevin Pietersen was England's captain during the infamous "Stanford Super Series," which was marred by controversy and financial scandal.

Did You Know?

1. Sir Jack Hobbs scored more first-class runs (61,760) and centuries (199) than any other player in history, a record that still stands today.
2. W.G. Grace played first-class cricket for over 44 seasons, from the age of 18 until he was 60, showcasing his extraordinary career longevity.
3. Andrew "Freddie" Flintoff was awarded the title of 'Man of the Series' in the 2005 Ashes, one of the most closely contested series ever, for his all-around performance.
4. James Anderson became the first fast bowler to take 600 Test wickets, solidifying his place among the greatest bowlers in the history of cricket.
5. In the 1981 Ashes series, Ian Botham became a national hero, especially after his incredible performance in the Headingley Test, where he turned the game around with both bat and ball.
6. Alastair Cook holds the record for the longest time spent batting in Test cricket for England, totaling over 625 hours at the crease throughout his career.
7. Joe Root reached 5,000 Test runs quicker than any other English player in history, demonstrating his prodigious batting talent early in his career.
8. After recovering from throat cancer, Geoffrey Boycott returned to Test cricket at the age of 39 and scored his 100th first-class century at Headingley in 1977, his home ground.
9. Graham Gooch's 333 runs against India at Lord's in 1990 is the highest Test score at the iconic ground by an English player.
10. Under Michael Vaughan's captaincy, England won 26 of their 51 Test matches, making him one of the most successful English captains by win percentage.

11. Stuart Broad took 8-15 against Australia in 2015, recording one of the fastest and most devastating bowling spells in Ashes history.
12. Kevin Pietersen was one of the first players to popularize the switch hit in international cricket, famously using it against New Zealand in 2008.
13. Tom Graveney was recalled to the England Test team at the age of 39 and went on to score over 2,000 runs in his late career, proving age is just a number.
14. Alec Stewart, who scored 8,463 Test runs for England, celebrated his 100th Test match by scoring a century against the West Indies on his birthday.

CHAPTER 3:
ICONIC CRICKET GROUNDS IN THE UK

1. What is the oldest cricket ground in the world that is still in use today?

    a. The Oval
    b. Lord's
    c. Old Trafford
    d. Trent Bridge

2. Which cricket ground is known as the "Home of Cricket"?

    a. The Oval
    b. Lord's
    c. Edgbaston
    d. Headingley

3. At which ground did Brian Lara score his record-breaking 501 not out in 1994?

    a. Trent Bridge
    b. Old Trafford
    c. Edgbaston
    d. Headingley

4. Where is the world-famous Ashes urn traditionally kept?

    a. MCC Museum at Lord's
    b. The Oval
    c. Edgbaston
    d. Trent Bridge

5. Which UK cricket ground is situated on the River Taff?
   a. Sophia Gardens, Cardiff
   b. Riverside Ground, Chester-le-Street
   c. The Rose Bowl, Southampton
   d. Taunton County Ground

6. In which city is the Headingley Cricket Ground located?
   a. Manchester
   b. Leeds
   c. Birmingham
   d. London

7. Which ground hosted the first-ever international test match in England?
   a. The Oval
   b. Lord's
   c. Old Trafford
   d. Trent Bridge

8. Which cricket ground is famous for the Botham Ashes Test of 1981?
   a. Edgbaston
   b. Headingley
   c. The Oval
   d. Lord's

9. Where did England secure their 2005 Ashes series victory?
   a. Trent Bridge
   b. The Oval
   c. Lord's
   d. Edgbaston

10. Which ground is known for the Western Terrace, famous for its lively atmosphere?
    a. Headingley
    b. The Oval
    c. Edgbaston
    d. Lord's

11. What is the capacity of Lord's Cricket Ground?
    a. 28,000
    b. 31,000
    c. 26,000
    d. 35,000

12. Which ground in London hosted the first-ever World Cup final in 1975?
    a. The Oval
    b. Lord's
    c. Kennington Oval
    d. All of the above

13. What unique feature distinguishes the Trent Bridge ground?
    a. It has a library within the ground.
    b. It is surrounded by a moat.
    c. It has the oldest pavilion in continuous use.
    d. It features a permanent balloon for aerial views.

14. Which ground is primarily the home of Glamorgan County Cricket Club?
    a. The SWALEC Stadium
    b. Riverside Ground
    c. Old Trafford
    d. Rose Bowl

15. What makes the Riverside Ground in Chester-le-Street unique?
    a. It has the largest playing surface.
    b. It is the northernmost first-class cricket ground in England.
    c. It is the newest Test cricket ground.
    d. It has a retractable roof.

16. Which ground is famously known as the fortress of Warwickshire County Cricket Club?
    a. Edgbaston
    b. The Oval
    c. Lord's
    d. Headingley

17. What is notable about the redevelopment of The Oval in the early 2000s?
    a. It was the first to install floodlights.
    b. It introduced the first retractable seating.
    c. It increased its capacity significantly.
    d. It added an underground cricket museum.

18. Which cricket ground in London hosted the 2019 World Cup final?
    a. The Oval
    b. Lord's
    c. Kennington Oval
    d. All of the above

19. Where did Shane Warne deliver the "Ball of the Century" in 1993?
    a. Old Trafford
    b. The Oval
    c. Lord's
    d. Edgbaston

20. Which ground is recognized for having the first thatched roof stand in the UK?
    a. Taunton County Ground
    b. Trent Bridge
    c. The Rose Bowl
    d. Riverside Ground

21. At which ground did England play their 1,000th Test match?
    a. Edgbaston
    b. Lord's
    c. The Oval
    d. Trent Bridge

22. Which ground in Nottingham is known for its historic pavilion and lush outfield?
    a. Trent Bridge
    b. Riverside Ground

c. Old Trafford
  d. The Oval

23. Which stadium was the first in England to host a day/night Test match?
    a. Edgbaston
    b. The Oval
    c. Lord's
    d. Trent Bridge

24. Where did James Anderson become the first fast bowler to reach 600 Test wickets?
    a. The Oval
    b. Lord's
    c. Old Trafford
    d. Edgbaston

25. Which ground is home to the National Cricket Academy?
    a. Lord's
    b. The Oval
    c. Loughborough
    d. Taunton

Quiz Answers

1. **D – Trent Bridge.** Trent Bridge is considered the oldest cricket ground in the world still in use today, having hosted games since the 1830s.
2. **B – Lord's.** Lord's is widely known as the "Home of Cricket," serving as a central hub for cricket since 1814.
3. **C – Edgbaston.** Brian Lara scored his record-breaking 501 not out in 1994 at Edgbaston, Birmingham.
4. **A – MCC Museum at Lord's.** The Ashes urn is traditionally kept at the MCC Museum within Lord's Cricket Ground.
5. **A – Sophia Gardens, Cardiff.** Sophia Gardens is situated on the River Taff and is known for hosting international cricket matches.
6. **B – Leeds.** Headingley Cricket Ground is located in Leeds, known for its rich cricket history.
7. **A – The Oval.** The Oval hosted the first-ever international test match in England in 1880 against Australia.
8. **B – Headingley.** The Botham Ashes Test of 1981, known for Ian Botham's remarkable performance, took place at Headingley.
9. **B – The Oval.** England secured their 2005 Ashes series victory at The Oval, with a memorable match concluding the series.
10. **A – Headingley.** Headingley is known for the Western Terrace, a spot famous for its lively and vibrant atmosphere.
11. **B – 31,000.** The capacity of Lord's Cricket Ground is 31,000, making it one of the largest cricket venues in the UK.
12. **B – Lord's.** Lord's hosted the first-ever World Cup final in 1975, marking a significant event in cricket history.
13. **C – It has the oldest pavilion in continuous use.** Trent Bridge is distinguished by having the oldest pavilion still in continuous use, dating back to its origins.
14. **A – The SWALEC Stadium.** The SWALEC Stadium, also known as Sophia Gardens, is primarily the home of Glamorgan County Cricket Club.
15. **B – It is the northernmost first-class cricket ground in England.** The Riverside Ground in Chester-le-Street is unique for being the northernmost first-class cricket ground in England.

16. **A – Edgbaston.** Edgbaston is famously known as the fortress of Warwickshire County Cricket Club, hosting many memorable matches.
17. **C – It increased its capacity significantly.** The Oval underwent significant redevelopment in the early 2000s, notably increasing its seating capacity.
18. **B – Lord's.** Lord's hosted the 2019 Cricket World Cup final, a significant event in the sport's recent history.
19. **A – Old Trafford.** Shane Warne delivered the "Ball of the Century" at Old Trafford during the 1993 Ashes series.
20. **A – Taunton County Ground.** Taunton County Ground is recognized for having one of the first thatched roof stands in the UK.
21. **A – Edgbaston.** England played their 1,000th Test match at Edgbaston, marking a significant milestone in their cricketing history.
22. **A – Trent Bridge.** Trent Bridge in Nottingham is known for its historic pavilion and lush outfield, making it a favorite among players and fans.
23. **A – Edgbaston.** Edgbaston was the first stadium in England to host a day/night Test match, adding a new dimension to Test cricket in the UK.
24. **C – Old Trafford.** James Anderson became the first fast bowler to reach 600 Test wickets at Old Trafford, cementing his place in cricket history.
25. **C – Loughborough.** Loughborough is home to the National Cricket Academy, serving as a training hub for upcoming cricket talent in England.

Did You Know?

1. Did you know that the pitch at Lord's has a distinct slope, falling 2.5 meters from the Pavilion end to the Nursery end, which can significantly affect the movement of the ball?
2. The iconic gas holders visible beyond the boundary at The Oval have become a symbol of the ground. They were granted Grade II listed status as landmarks of industrial history.

3. Unique among international cricket grounds, Headingley features twin sightscreens at one end of the pitch to accommodate the bowler's run-up from either side.
4. Edgbaston was the first English ground outside London to host an international test match, beginning its storied Test history in 1902.
5. Trent Bridge got its name from the nearby "Trent Bridge" over the River Trent, which is a notable architectural feature and has been a part of Nottingham since 1871.
6. During World War II, Old Trafford suffered significant bomb damage, which led to no Test cricket being played there between 1939 and 1945.
7. The Ageas Bowl is renowned for its modern, amphitheater-like design, which provides uninterrupted views from every seat, making it one of the most spectator-friendly grounds in the country.
8. Sophia Gardens is not just famous for cricket but also for its scenic location next to the River Taff, adding to the picturesque setting for spectators.
9. The Riverside Ground in Chester-le-Street offers views of the historic Lumley Castle, creating a dramatic backdrop for cricket matches.
10. During World War I, anti-aircraft guns were positioned at The Oval to help defend London against Zeppelin raids.
11. The futuristic J.P. Morgan Media Centre at Lord's, opened in 1999, won the RIBA Stirling Prize for architecture and has become an iconic feature of the ground.
12. Edgbaston hosted the first-ever floodlit cricket match in Britain in 1997, a pioneering moment for night games in the country.
13. Trent Bridge holds the record for the smallest margin of victory by runs in an Ashes Test, with England beating Australia by just 3 runs in 1926.
14. After a fire in 1932 destroyed the main stand, Headingley was quickly rebuilt and reopened the following year, showcasing the community's commitment to cricket.
15. The Oval was one of the 15 venues for the first Cricket World Cup in 1975 and has hosted key matches in every subsequent UK-hosted World Cup.

CHAPTER 4:
THE ASHES - A HISTORIC RIVALRY

1. In what year was the first Ashes series played?
    a. 1882
    b. 1892
    c. 1902
    d. 1912

2. What is the Ashes urn traditionally believed to contain?
    a. A piece of a cricket ball
    b. A bail
    c. Ashes of a wooden bail
    d. Ashes of a cricket stump

3. Which ground is traditionally the venue for the final Test of an Ashes series in England?
    a. Lord's
    b. The Oval
    c. Edgbaston
    d. Old Trafford

4. Who was the England captain during the famous 2005 Ashes series?
    a. Michael Vaughan
    b. Andrew Flintoff
    c. Alastair Cook
    d. Kevin Pietersen

5. Which Australian bowler famously delivered the "Ball of the Century" during the 1993 Ashes series?

a. Brett Lee
   b. Glenn McGrath
   c. Shane Warne
   d. Dennis Lillee

6. Who scored the highest individual score in an Ashes series?

   a. Don Bradman
   b. Steve Smith
   c. Len Hutton
   d. Ricky Ponting

7. Which player holds the record for the most runs in Ashes history?

   a. Sir Donald Bradman
   b. Sir Jack Hobbs
   c. Sir Alastair Cook
   d. Steve Waugh

8. Who is the youngest player ever to play in the Ashes?

   a. Sachin Tendulkar
   b. Ben Hollioake
   c. Doug Walters
   d. Ian Botham

9. What significant event happened during the 1932-1933 Ashes series?

   a. Introduction of One-Day Internationals
   b. The Bodyline tactics were employed
   c. The series was cancelled due to war
   d. The debut of colored clothing in Tests

10. Who has taken the most wickets in Ashes history?

    a. Shane Warne
    b. Glenn McGrath
    c. Stuart Broad
    d. James Anderson

11. Which English batsman famously batted with a broken arm in the Ashes?

    a. Colin Cowdrey
    b. Ian Botham
    c. Mike Atherton
    d. Geoffrey Boycott

12. In which year did England last win the Ashes series?

    a. 2015
    b. 2017
    c. 2018
    d. 2019

13. What unique record did Reggie Duff achieve in his debut Ashes match?

    a. Fastest fifty
    b. Century on debut
    c. Most wickets in an innings by a debutant
    d. Hat-trick on debut

14. Which Ashes series is known for having all five Tests drawn?

    a. The 1970-71 series
    b. The 1962-63 series
    c. The 1974-75 series
    d. The 1986-87 series

15. Who was the first bowler to take 300 Ashes wickets?

    a. Dennis Lillee
    b. Shane Warne
    c. Stuart Broad
    d. Glenn McGrath

16. How many times has the Ashes series been played as of 2021?

    a. 71 series
    b. 72 series
    c. 70 series
    d. 73 series

17. What was the shortest completed Ashes Test match in terms of days?

    a. 2 days
    b. 3 days
    c. 4 days
    d. 5 days

18. Who captained Australia to their first Ashes victory on English soil?

    a. Warwick Armstrong
    b. Allan Border
    c. Don Bradman
    d. Steve Waugh

19. Which player scored a century in both his first and last Ashes Tests?

    a. Greg Chappell
    b. Geoffrey Boycott
    c. David Gower
    d. Ricky Ponting

20. Which English city hosted the first-ever Ashes Test?

    a. London
    b. Manchester
    c. Birmingham
    d. Leeds

21. What is the highest successful run chase in an Ashes Test at The Oval?

    a. 263 runs
    b. 322 runs
    c. 289 runs
    d. 359 runs

22. Who was the leading wicket-taker in the 2005 Ashes series?

    a. Shane Warne
    b. Andrew Flintoff

c. Brett Lee
   d. Simon Jones

23. Which pair holds the record for the highest partnership in Ashes history?
    a. Don Bradman and Bill Ponsford
    b. Steve Waugh and Ricky Ponting
    c. Alastair Cook and Jonathan Trott
    d. Jack Hobbs and Herbert Sutcliffe

24. What year was the Ashes series first broadcast on television?
    a. 1938
    b. 1953
    c. 1948
    d. 1960

25. Who was the first player to score 400 runs and take 10 wickets in a single Ashes series?
    a. Ian Botham
    b. Andrew Flintoff
    c. Ben Stokes
    d. Gary Sobers

Quiz Answers

1. **A – 1882.** The first Ashes series was played in 1882, marking the beginning of one of cricket's most celebrated rivalries between England and Australia.
2. **C – Ashes of a wooden bail.** The Ashes urn is traditionally believed to contain the ashes of a wooden bail, symbolizing the "death" of English cricket.
3. **B – The Oval.** The Oval is traditionally the venue for the final Test of an Ashes series in England, often deciding the outcome of the series.
4. **A – Michael Vaughan.** Michael Vaughan was the England captain during the famous 2005 Ashes series, leading his team to a memorable victory.
5. **C – Shane Warne.** Shane Warne, the Australian bowler, famously delivered the "Ball of the Century" during the 1993 Ashes series.
6. **C – Len Hutton.** Len Hutton scored the highest individual score in an Ashes series with 364 runs in 1938.)
7. **A – Sir Donald Bradman.** Sir Donald Bradman holds the record for the most runs in Ashes history, a testament to his legendary status in cricket.
8. **C – Doug Walters.** Doug Walters is noted as the youngest player ever to play in the Ashes, debuting at a very young age.
9. **B – The Bodyline tactics were employed.** During the 1932-1933 Ashes series, the infamous Bodyline tactics were employed by England, causing significant controversy and strain in Anglo-Australian cricket relations.
10. **A – Shane Warne.** Shane Warne has taken the most wickets in Ashes history, making him one of the most successful bowlers in the history of this storied series.
11. **A – Colin Cowdrey.** Colin Cowdrey famously batted with a broken arm in the Ashes, showcasing incredible bravery and commitment to his team.
12. **A – 2015.** England last won the Ashes series in 2015, regaining the urn on home soil.

13. **B – Century on debut.** Reggie Duff achieved the unique record of scoring a century on his debut in an Ashes match, making an immediate impact.
14. **B – The 1962-63 series.** The 1962-63 Ashes series is known for having all five Tests drawn, a rare occurrence in the history of this intense rivalry.
15. **B – Shane Warne.** Shane Warne was the first bowler to take 300 Ashes wickets, further cementing his legacy as one of the greatest spin bowlers of all time.
16. **A – 71 series.** As of 2021, the Ashes series has been played 71 times, with a rich history dating back to 1882.
17. **A – 2 days.** The shortest completed Ashes Test match, in terms of days, lasted only 2 days, reflecting the dominant performances that can occur in Test cricket.
18. **A – Warwick Armstrong.** Warwick Armstrong captained Australia to their first Ashes victory on English soil, leading a strong team that overcame the English challenge.
19. **A – Greg Chappell.** Greg Chappell scored a century in both his first and last Ashes Tests, a remarkable feat that highlights his consistent performance throughout his career.
20. **B – Manchester.** The first-ever Ashes Test was hosted in Manchester, at Old Trafford, one of cricket's most historic venues.
21. **B – 322 runs.** The highest successful run chase in an Ashes Test at The Oval is 322 runs, showcasing the potential for exciting finishes at this iconic venue.
22. **D – Simon Jones.** Simon Jones was the leading wicket-taker in the 2005 Ashes series, playing a pivotal role in England's series victory.
23. **A – Don Bradman and Bill Ponsford.** Don Bradman and Bill Ponsford hold the record for the highest partnership in Ashes history, combining for a monumental partnership that underscored their batting prowess.
24. **A – 1938.** The Ashes series was first broadcast on television in 1938, allowing fans to watch the matches live and bringing the series to a wider audience.
25. **A – Ian Botham.** Ian Botham was the first player to score 400 runs and take 10 wickets in a single Ashes series, demonstrating his legendary all-round capabilities.

Did You Know?

1. The term "The Ashes" was first used after Australia defeated England in 1882 at The Oval, leading to a satirical obituary in The Sporting Times that declared the death of English cricket, stating that the body would be cremated and the ashes taken to Australia.
2. The Ashes urn is a small terracotta artifact, only 11 cm high, and was originally a personal gift to England captain Ivo Bligh during the 1882-83 series.
3. Did you know that the first recognized series of Test matches between English and Australian women's teams was played in 1934-35?
4. The 1932-33 Ashes series, known as the "Bodyline Series" due to England's controversial bowling tactics, is one of the most infamous cricket series ever played, which strained diplomatic relations between England and Australia.
5. The Ashes series was first televised during England's tour of Australia in 1958-59, marking a significant milestone in bringing cricket into homes around the world.
6. In March 1977, exactly 100 years after the first Test was played, a Centenary Test was held at Melbourne Cricket Ground, and incredibly, Australia won by the same margin as the first match—45 runs.
7. The longest gap between any two Ashes series was from 1975 to 1977, due to the introduction of World Series Cricket.
8. During the 2010-11 Ashes series, the Melbourne Cricket Ground (MCG) witnessed a record attendance of 91,092 on the first day of the Boxing Day Test, the highest-ever crowd at a day of Test cricket.
9. In 2002, England captain Nasser Hussain famously decided to field first at the Gabba, and then was dismissed for a golden duck in the first innings.
10. The first-ever day/night Test match in Ashes history took place at the Adelaide Oval during the 2017-18 series, a testament to the evolving nature of Test cricket.

11. Bob Simpson, in his comeback series aged 41, scored a double century during the 1977-78 Ashes after having retired for nearly a decade.
12. The first hat-trick in Ashes history was taken by Australian Fred Spofforth, also known as "The Demon Bowler," during the inaugural 1878-79 series.
13. The 2005 Ashes series saw the first instance in Ashes history where all 11 players of a team were out caught in a single innings (England's second innings at Trent Bridge).

CHAPTER 5:
GREAT CRICKET RIVALRIES

1. Which two teams compete in the fiercely contested India-Pakistan cricket rivalry?

    a. India vs. Bangladesh
    b. India vs. Sri Lanka
    c. India vs. Pakistan
    d. Pakistan vs. Afghanistan

2. The "Battle of the Blues" is a historic cricket rivalry between which two universities?

    a. Harvard vs. Yale
    b. Oxford vs. Cambridge
    c. Princeton vs. Stanford
    d. MIT vs. Caltech

3. Which rivalry is known as the "Trans-Tasman Trophy"?

    a. Australia vs. New Zealand
    b. Australia vs. South Africa
    c. New Zealand vs. South Africa
    d. England vs. New Zealand

4. The "Calcutta Cup" is contested in rugby between which two nations?

    a. India and Bangladesh
    b. Scotland and England
    c. Australia and New Zealand
    d. Ireland and Wales

5. Which Caribbean island rivalry is known for its intense competition in regional cricket?

    a. Barbados vs. Trinidad and Tobago
    b. Jamaica vs. Barbados
    c. Trinidad and Tobago vs. Guyana
    d. Jamaica vs. Guyana

6. The "Border-Gavaskar Trophy" is contested between which two cricket teams?

    a. India and Pakistan
    b. Australia and India
    c. Australia and South Africa
    d. England and India

7. What is the historic cricket rivalry between South Africa and Australia known as?

    a. Freedom Series
    b. Proteas Challenge
    c. Southern Derby
    d. None of the above

8. Which country does England compete against in the "Basil D'Oliveira Trophy"?

    a. India
    b. West Indies
    c. South Africa
    d. Australia

9. The "Chappell-Hadlee Trophy" is contested between which two cricket teams?

    a. Australia and New Zealand
    b. Australia and England
    c. New Zealand and South Africa
    d. England and New Zealand

10. What is the rivalry between Sri Lanka and India commonly referred to as?

a. Emerald Battle
b. Asian Derby
c. Subcontinental Clash
d. Cricketing Neighbors

11. The "Rose Bowl" is the name of the cricket ground associated with which English county rivalry?

    a. Lancashire vs. Yorkshire
    b. Hampshire vs. Surrey
    c. Middlesex vs. Surrey
    d. Kent vs. Surrey

12. Which two teams play for the "Wisden Trophy"?

    a. England and India
    b. West Indies and India
    c. England and West Indies
    d. Australia and West Indies

13. What is the fierce rivalry between South African provincial teams Cape Cobras and Dolphins known as?

    a. Cape Battle
    b. Coastal Derby
    c. Proteas Pride
    d. Southern Smash

14. The "Sheffield Shield" is a domestic competition in which country?

    a. England
    b. Australia
    c. South Africa
    d. New Zealand

15. Which two county teams are involved in the "War of the Roses" cricket rivalry?

    a. Lancashire and Yorkshire
    b. Essex and Kent
    c. Sussex and Surrey
    d. Gloucestershire and Somerset

16. The rivalry between which two teams is sometimes referred to as the "Battle for the Bails"?
    a. India and Pakistan
    b. England and Australia
    c. South Africa and Australia
    d. New Zealand and Australia

17. Which international rivalry is known for the "Sir Vivian Richards Trophy"?
    a. England vs. West Indies
    b. Australia vs. West Indies
    c. South Africa vs. West Indies
    d. India vs. West Indies

18. The "Moin-ud-Dowlah Gold Cup" is associated with which country's domestic cricket?
    a. Pakistan
    b. India
    c. Bangladesh
    d. Sri Lanka

19. Which two teams compete for the "KFC Big Bash League" rivalry in Australia?
    e. Sydney Thunder vs. Sydney Sixers
    f. Melbourne Stars vs. Melbourne Renegades
    g. Brisbane Heat vs. Adelaide Strikers
    h. Perth Scorchers vs. Hobart Hurricanes

20. Which international cricket competitions feature matches between Pakistan and Bangladesh?
    a. Asia Cup
    b. ICC World Cup
    c. ICC T20 World Cup
    d. All of the above

21. The "Desert Derby" refers to the rivalry between which two teams?

a. UAE and Oman
   b. UAE and Qatar
   c. Saudi Arabia and Oman
   d. Qatar and Bahrain

22. Which trophy is contested between Australia and South Africa in Test cricket?
   a. Mandela Trophy
   b. Freedom Series
   c. Rainbow Trophy
   d. Proteas-Aussie Trophy

23. What marks the cricket rivalry between India and Bangladesh in international tournaments?
   a. Close finishes in ICC events
   b. Notable upsets by Bangladesh
   c. Competitive spirit despite differences in historical success
   d. All of the above

24. The intense cricket rivalry between which two English counties is often just referred to as the "Local Derby"?
   a. Kent vs. Essex
   b. Surrey vs. Middlesex
   c. Nottinghamshire vs. Derbyshire
   d. Lancashire vs. Cheshire

25. What annual competition between English public schools features a rivalry over 200 years old?
   a. Eton vs. Harrow
   b. Winchester vs. Charterhouse
   c. Rugby vs. Marlborough
   d. Westminster vs. St Paul's

Quiz Answers

1. **C – India vs. Pakistan.** The India-Pakistan cricket rivalry is one of the most intense and fiercely contested in the sport, known for its passionate fans and historic significance.
2. **B – Oxford vs. Cambridge.** The "Battle of the Blues" refers to the historic cricket rivalry between Oxford and Cambridge universities, a traditional contest that dates back to the 19th century.
3. **A – Australia vs. New Zealand.** The "Trans-Tasman Trophy" is the name given to the cricket rivalry between Australia and New Zealand, named after the Tasman Sea that separates the two countries.
4. **B – Scotland and England.** The "Calcutta Cup" is contested in rugby between Scotland and England, one of the oldest rivalries in the sport, originating from the Calcutta Rugby Football Club in India.
5. **A – Barbados vs. Trinidad and Tobago.** This Caribbean island rivalry between Barbados and Trinidad and Tobago is known for its intense competition in regional cricket, often featuring highly competitive matches.
6. **B – Australia and India.** The "Border-Gavaskar Trophy" is contested between Australia and India, named after two of the cricketing legends from these countries, Allan Border and Sunil Gavaskar.
7. **D – None of the above.** The historic cricket rivalry between South Africa and Australia does not have a specific name like the Freedom Series or others listed, but is simply known for its competitive nature.
8. **C – South Africa.** England competes against South Africa in the "Basil D'Oliveira Trophy," named after the cricketer who was born in South Africa and played for England, symbolizing significant historical and social implications.
9. **A – Australia and New Zealand.** The "Chappell-Hadlee Trophy" is contested between Australia and New Zealand, named after two famous cricketing families from these countries, the Chappells and the Hadlees.

10. **C – Subcontinental Clash.** The rivalry between Sri Lanka and India in cricket is commonly referred to as the "Subcontinental Clash," highlighting the geographical and competitive nature of matches between these neighbors.
11. **B – Hampshire vs. Surrey.** The Rose Bowl, now known as the Ageas Bowl, is the cricket ground associated with Hampshire and has seen many memorable clashes with Surrey.
12. **C – England and West Indies.** The "Wisden Trophy" was played for between England and West Indies, one of the long-standing and historic rivalries in cricket.
13. **B – Coastal Derby.** The fierce rivalry between South African provincial teams Cape Cobras and Dolphins is known as the "Coastal Derby," highlighting the regional competition along South Africa's coastlines.
14. **B – Australia.** The "Sheffield Shield" is a domestic competition in Australia, involving state teams in a first-class cricket format, recognized as one of the premier domestic cricket competitions worldwide.
15. **A – Lancashire and Yorkshire.** The "War of the Roses" cricket rivalry between Lancashire and Yorkshire is named after the historical civil wars in England between the House of Lancaster and the House of York.
16. **B – England and Australia.** The rivalry between England and Australia, particularly in the Ashes context, is sometimes referred to as the "Battle for the Bails."
17. **A – England vs. West Indies.** The "Sir Vivian Richards Trophy" is contested between England and West Indies, named after one of the greatest cricketers from the West Indies, Sir Vivian Richards.
18. **B – India.** The "Moin-ud-Dowlah Gold Cup" is associated with India's domestic cricket, a prestigious tournament played primarily by state teams and institutions.
19. **B – Melbourne Stars vs. Melbourne Renegades.** In the "KFC Big Bash League," the rivalry between Melbourne Stars and Melbourne Renegades is especially fierce, known for its city derby atmosphere.

20. **D. All of the above**. Pakistan and Bangladesh frequently compete in these major international tournaments, reflecting their ongoing cricket rivalry.
21. **A – UAE and Oman.** The "Desert Derby" refers to the rivalry between UAE and Oman, highlighting regional competition in the Gulf area.
22. **B – Freedom Series.** The trophy contested between Australia and South Africa in Test cricket is known as the "Freedom Series," symbolizing the post-apartheid era friendship and competitive spirit between the two nations.
23. **D. All of the above.** The cricket encounters between India and Bangladesh in international tournaments are known for their competitive matches, occasional upsets by Bangladesh, and close finishes, highlighting their growing rivalry.
24. **C – Nottinghamshire vs. Derbyshire.** The intense cricket rivalry between Nottinghamshire and Derbyshire is often just referred to as the "Local Derby," marking the geographical closeness and traditional rivalry of the teams.
25. **A – Eton vs. Harrow.** The annual competition between English public schools Eton and Harrow features a rivalry over 200 years old, showcasing a deep-rooted tradition in cricket education.

Did You Know?

1. The India-Pakistan rivalry is not just fierce competition; it often brings diplomatic gestures, such as players from both teams sharing meals and exchanging jerseys, symbolizing peace and sportsmanship.
2. The Oxford vs. Cambridge University cricket match, also known as the University Match, has been played at Lord's Cricket Ground since 1827, making it one of the oldest annual fixtures at this iconic venue.
3. The first-ever day/night Test match in the Trans-Tasman Trophy series was played at Adelaide Oval in 2015, marking a new era in the storied rivalry between Australia and New Zealand.
4. The annual Eton vs. Harrow cricket match is one of the longest-running sporting fixtures in the world, with the first match played back in 1805.
5. The Freedom Series between South Africa and India symbolizes the end of apartheid, celebrating South Africa's return to international cricket in 1991 with their tour of India.
6. This trophy is named after a cricketer whose selection controversy in 1968 led to the cancellation of a South Africa-England series, significantly impacting international cricket relations.
7. The Women's Ashes was officially recognized in 1998, although women's Ashes contests date back to 1934-35, highlighting the longstanding competitive spirit between the women's teams of England and Australia.
8. The Chappell-Hadlee Trophy, awarded in the one-day series between Australia and New Zealand, is named after the Chappell brothers of Australia and Sir Richard Hadlee of New Zealand, emphasizing the familial ties across the rivalry.
9. The India vs. Pakistan cricket matches are some of the most-watched television events in both countries, often bringing everyday activities to a standstill as millions tune in.
10. The Calcutta Cup, a rugby trophy contested between England and Scotland, originated from the Calcutta (now Kolkata)

Cricket Club after it disbanded, and the funds were used to create the trophy.
11. Matches between India and Pakistan often draw record crowds, with the 1999 World Cup encounter at Old Trafford witnessing one of the largest audiences for a non-final match.
12. The Bodyline series, also known as the 1932-33 Ashes series, involved tactics that were not only controversial on the field but also strained diplomatic relations between England and Australia.
13. The Sir Vivian Richards Trophy, contested between England and West Indies, is named after one of cricket's greatest batsmen, Sir Vivian Richards, symbolizing respect and admiration across nations.
14. The Sheffield Shield, one of the oldest cricket competitions in Australia, was originally known as the Inter-Colonial Tournament when it was established in 1892-93, showcasing the deep-rooted regional rivalries within Australian cricket.

CHAPTER 6:
WORLD CUP WONDERS

1. Which country won the first ever Cricket World Cup in 1975?
   a. Australia
   b. West Indies
   c. England
   d. India

2. Who scored the highest individual score in a single World Cup match?
   a. Sachin Tendulkar
   b. Martin Guptill
   c. Chris Gayle
   d. Rohit Sharma

3. Which bowler has the best bowling figures in a World Cup match?
   a. Glenn McGrath
   b. Wasim Akram
   c. Muttiah Muralitharan
   d. Glenn Turner

4. What is the highest team score in a World Cup match?
   a. 413-5 by India
   b. 417-6 by Australia
   c. 398-5 by South Africa
   d. 408-5 by Sri Lanka

5. Which player has won the most World Cup titles as a captain?

a. Clive Lloyd
   b. Ricky Ponting
   c. Allan Border
   d. Arjuna Ranatunga

6. Who hit the winning runs for India in the 2011 World Cup final?

   a. Yuvraj Singh
   b. MS Dhoni
   c. Gautam Gambhir
   d. Virat Kohli

7. Which country hosted the Cricket World Cup for the first time in 1987?

   a. Australia and New Zealand
   b. England
   c. India and Pakistan
   d. West Indies

8. Who is the only player to score a century in both a World Cup semi-final and final?

   a. Vivian Richards
   b. Sachin Tendulkar
   c. Mahela Jayawardene
   d. Ricky Ponting

9. What was the total number of teams that participated in the 1975 World Cup?

   a. 8
   b. 10
   c. 12
   d. 14

10. Which player holds the record for the most wickets in a single World Cup tournament?

    a. Mitchell Starc
    b. Glenn McGrath
    c. Shaheen Afridi
    d. Shane Warne

11. In which year did the Cricket World Cup feature a Super Six stage?

    a. 1992
    b. 1996
    c. 1999
    d. 2003

12. Which player scored the fastest century in World Cup history?

    a. AB de Villiers
    b. Kevin O'Brien
    c. Corey Anderson
    d. Chris Gayle

13. Which team won the World Cup in 1996?

    a. Australia
    b. Sri Lanka
    c. India
    d. Pakistan

14. What is the record for the highest number of runs scored by an individual in a single World Cup tournament?

    a. 673 by Sachin Tendulkar
    b. 658 by Matthew Hayden
    c. 606 by Mahela Jayawardene
    d. 734 by Kane Williamson

15. Which team has appeared in the most World Cup finals without ever winning the title?

    a. England
    b. New Zealand
    c. South Africa
    d. Kenya

16. How many consecutive World Cup matches did Australia win between 1999 and 2011?

    a. 25
    b. 27

c. 29
d. 34

17. Who is the youngest player to ever win a Cricket World Cup?
    a. Sachin Tendulkar
    b. Ben Stokes
    c. Waqar Younis
    d. Inzamam-ul-Haq

18. Which country was the first to win the Cricket World Cup on home soil?
    a. India
    b. Australia
    c. England
    d. West Indies

19. Who is the oldest player to have played in a World Cup final?
    a. Imran Khan
    b. Sachin Tendulkar
    c. Misbah-ul-Haq
    d. Muttiah Muralitharan

20. Which player holds the record for scoring the most half-centuries in World Cup history?
    e. Kumar Sangakkara
    f. Sachin Tendulkar
    g. Ricky Ponting
    h. AB de Villiers

21. Which country reached the semi-finals in their debut appearance at the Cricket World Cup?
    a. Sri Lanka
    b. Bangladesh
    c. South Africa
    d. Afghanistan

22. Who captained the West Indies to their first two World Cup victories?

a. Sir Viv Richards
b. Brian Lara
c. Clive Lloyd
d. Chris Gayle

23. What unique record did India achieve in the 1983 World Cup?
    a. They defeated the defending champions in the final.
    b. They won all their matches.
    c. They had the highest run-scorer and wicket-taker.
    d. They played the maximum number of matches.

24. Which bowler took a hat-trick in a World Cup final?
    a. Wasim Akram
    b. Mitchell Starc
    c. Lasith Malinga
    d. Adam Gilchrist (non-bowler option for trick question)

25. How many times has the World Cup been held in the southern hemisphere?
    a. 3
    b. 4
    c. 5
    d. 6

Quiz Answers

1. **B – West Indies.** The West Indies won the first ever Cricket World Cup in 1975, defeating Australia in the final.
2. **B. Martin Guptill.** Martin Guptill holds the record for the highest individual score in a World Cup match. During the 2015 ICC Cricket World Cup, Guptill scored an unbeaten 237 runs off 163 balls in the quarterfinal match against West Indies. This monumental innings included 24 fours and 11 sixes, making it not only the highest score in World Cup history but also the second-highest score in all One Day Internationals (ODIs) at the time. This performance was instrumental in New Zealand's victory in that match, and it remains a standout achievement in World Cup history.
3. **A – Glenn McGrath.** Glenn McGrath holds the record for the best bowling figures in a World Cup match, taking 7 wickets for 15 runs.
4. **B – 417-6 by Australia.** Australia set the highest team score in a World Cup match, scoring 417-6 against Afghanistan in 2015.
5. **A – Clive Lloyd.** Clive Lloyd won the most World Cup titles as a captain, leading West Indies to victories in 1975 and 1979.
6. **B – MS Dhoni.** MS Dhoni hit the winning runs for India in the 2011 World Cup final against Sri Lanka.
7. **C – India and Pakistan.** The Cricket World Cup was hosted for the first time by India and Pakistan in 1987.
8. **C – Mahela Jayawardene.** Mahela Jayawardene is the only player to score a century in both a World Cup semi-final and final.
9. **A – 8.** The total number of teams that participated in the 1975 World Cup was 8.
10. **A – Mitchell Starc.** Mitchell Starc holds the record for the most wickets in a single World Cup tournament, taking 27 wickets in 2015.
11. **C – 1999.** The Cricket World Cup featured a Super Six stage for the first time in 1999.
12. **B – Kevin O'Brien.** Kevin O'Brien scored the fastest century in World Cup history, reaching the milestone in just 50 balls in 2011.

13. **B – Sri Lanka.** Sri Lanka won the World Cup in 1996, defeating Australia in the final.
14. **A – 673 by Sachin Tendulkarn.** He holds the record for the highest individual score in a World Cup match. He scored 673 runs during the 2003 ICC Cricket World Cup, the most by any player in a single tournament.
15. **B – New Zealand.** New Zealand has appeared in the most World Cup finals without ever winning the title, with losses in 2015 and 2019 among others.
16. **A – 25.** The winning streak began with their victory in the 1999 World Cup, continued through their undefeated campaigns in 2003 and 2007, where they won the tournament each time, and ended during the 2011 World Cup when they lost to Pakistan.
17. **D – Inzamam-ul-Haq.** Inzamam-ul-Haq is the youngest player to ever win a Cricket World Cup, being part of the Pakistan team that won in 1992.
18. **A – India.** India was the first country to win the Cricket World Cup on home soil, achieving this feat in 2011.
19. **A – Imran Khan.** Imran Khan is the oldest player to have played in a World Cup final, leading Pakistan to victory in 1992.
20. **B – Sachin Tendulkar.** Sachin Tendulkar holds the record for the most World Cup half-centuries, scoring 21 across his appearances from 1992 to 2011.
21. **C. South Africa.** South Africa reached the semi-finals in their debut World Cup appearance in 1992, showcasing a strong performance in their first tournament.
22. **C – Clive Lloyd.** Clive Lloyd captained the West Indies to their first two World Cup victories in 1975 and 1979.
23. **A – They defeated the defending champions in the final.** India achieved the unique record of defeating the defending champions West Indies in the 1983 World Cup final.
24. **C – Lasith Malinga.** Lasith Malinga took a hat-trick in the 2007 World Cup, though not in the final, he is the only one among the options to have taken a World Cup hat-trick.
25. **C – 5.** The World Cup has been held 5 times in the southern hemisphere: 1992, 2003, 2007, 2015, and 2023 shared by India.

Did You Know?

1. The inaugural World Cup was sponsored by Prudential Assurance Company and was officially called the Prudential Cup.
2. Until 1987, all World Cup matches were played in traditional white clothing and with red cricket balls.
3. The 1987 Cricket World Cup, co-hosted by India and Pakistan, was the first to be held outside England.
4. The 1992 World Cup introduced colored team uniforms and white cricket balls for the first time in history.
5. In the 1996 World Cup, Sri Lanka's aggressive top-order batting strategy revolutionized how the opening overs are played in limited-overs cricket.
6. Australia has won the World Cup five times, the most by any team, with their wins coming in 1987, 1999, 2003, 2007, and 2015.
7. The 1999 World Cup featured one of the greatest matches in cricket history, where Australia tied with South Africa in the semi-final but advanced to the final on superior run rate.
8. The 2019 World Cup final is widely regarded as one of the most dramatic cricket matches ever played, ending in a tie, followed by a tied Super Over, with England winning on boundary count.
9. Sachin Tendulkar holds the record for the most runs in World Cup history, scoring 2,278 runs across six World Cups.
10. The 2003 World Cup, held in South Africa, Zimbabwe, and Kenya, was the first to feature matches in Africa.
11. Ireland's Kevin O'Brien scored the fastest century in World Cup history in 2011, reaching 100 runs from just 50 balls against England.
12. The 1979 World Cup saw the introduction of the Man of the Match award in the final, with Viv Richards receiving the honor for his spectacular century.
13. The highest ever World Cup team total is 417-6, scored by Australia against Afghanistan in 2015.

14. New Zealand has reached the World Cup final three times but has yet to win the trophy, making them one of the most consistent yet unfortunate teams in the tournament's history.

CHAPTER 7:

MEMORABLE MATCHES

1. Which match is known as the "Greatest Test Match of the 20th Century"?

    a. England vs. Australia, 2005 Ashes, Edgbaston
    b. Australia vs. West Indies, 1960, Brisbane
    c. India vs. Australia, 2001, Kolkata
    d. Pakistan vs. India, 1999, Chennai

2. In which match did Anil Kumble take all ten wickets in an innings?

    a. India vs. Pakistan, Delhi, 1999
    b. India vs. Australia, Mumbai, 2004
    c. India vs. England, Kolkata, 1993
    d. India vs. West Indies, Chennai, 1994

3. What is the highest successful run chase in the history of Test cricket?

    a. 418 by West Indies vs. Australia, 2003
    b. 406 by India vs. West Indies, 1976
    c. 438 by South Africa vs. Australia, 2008
    d. 414 by South Africa vs. Australia, 2008

4. Which World Cup final was decided by a Super Over?

    a. 1999, England vs. Pakistan
    b. 2003, Australia vs. India
    c. 2019, England vs. New Zealand
    d. 2015, Australia vs. New Zealand

5. Which match is famous for Brian Lara's record-breaking 400 not out?

    a. West Indies vs. England, Antigua, 2004
    b. West Indies vs. Australia, Kingston, 1999
    c. West Indies vs. South Africa, Bridgetown, 2001
    d. West Indies vs. England, Barbados, 1999

6. Who hit the winning runs in the T20 World Cup Final in 2016?

    a. Carlos Brathwaite
    b. Marlon Samuels
    c. Ben Stokes
    d. Andre Russell

7. In which match did South Africa need 22 runs from 1 ball due to a rain rule miscalculation?

    a. 1992 World Cup Semi-final vs. England
    b. 1999 World Cup Semi-final vs. Australia
    c. 2003 World Cup group stage vs. Sri Lanka
    d. 2007 World Cup Semi-final vs. Australia

8. Which match featured the first-ever tied Test in the history of cricket?

    a. Australia vs. West Indies, Brisbane, 1960
    b. India vs. Pakistan, Kolkata, 1956
    c. England vs. Australia, Lord's, 1964
    d. South Africa vs. Australia, Johannesburg, 1952

9. What was the lowest total successfully defended in an ODI World Cup match?

    a. 125 by Zimbabwe vs. Australia
    b. 129 by Australia vs. West Indies
    c. 134 by Sri Lanka vs. New Zealand
    d. 143 by Zimbabwe vs. England

10. Who bowled the final over in the 2007 World T20 final?

    a. Misbah-ul-Haq
    b. Joginder Sharma

c. Shahid Afridi
d. Lasith Malinga

11. Which Test match saw the highest number of runs scored in a single game?
    a. England vs. Australia, 1938
    b. Sri Lanka vs. India, 1997
    c. West Indies vs. England, 1950
    d. South Africa vs. England, 1939

12. Who scored the fastest century in World Cup history?
    a. Kevin O'Brien
    b. AB de Villiers
    c. Glenn Maxwell
    d. Viv Richards

13. Which match was known for Shane Warne's "Ball of the Century"?
    a. Australia vs. England, Old Trafford, 1993
    b. Australia vs. South Africa, Sydney, 1994
    c. Australia vs. India, Melbourne, 1995
    d. Australia vs. New Zealand, Perth, 1997

14. What was the highest scoring ODI match ever played?
    a. India vs. Australia, Bangalore, 2013
    b. South Africa vs. Australia, Johannesburg, 2006
    c. England vs. Australia, Trent Bridge, 2018
    d. New Zealand vs. Australia, Hamilton, 2007

15. Which match saw the highest ever Test partnership of 624 runs?
    a. Kumar Sangakkara and Mahela Jayawardene vs. South Africa, Colombo, 2006
    b. Rahul Dravid and VVS Laxman vs. Australia, Kolkata, 2001
    c. Sanath Jayasuriya and Roshan Mahanama vs. India, Colombo, 1997
    d. Matthew Hayden and Justin Langer vs. Zimbabwe, Perth, 2003

16. Which ICC World Cup final saw Australia win by the largest margin by runs?

    a. 1999 vs. Pakistan
    b. 2003 vs. India
    c. 2007 vs. Sri Lanka
    d. 2015 vs. New Zealand

17. Who scored a double century in a Women's ODI World Cup?

    a. Belinda Clark
    b. Charlotte Edwards
    c. Mithali Raj
    d. Sarah Taylor

18. What was unique about the 1960 tied Test match between Australia and West Indies?

    a. It was the first-ever Test match broadcast on television.
    b. It was the first Test match to be completed in three days.
    c. It was the first-ever Test match to end in a tie.
    d. It featured the highest individual score in a debut match.

19. In which World Cup did Ireland defeat England, marking one of the biggest upsets in cricket history?

    a. 2007 World Cup in the West Indies
    b. 2011 World Cup in India, Sri Lanka, and Bangladesh
    c. 2015 World Cup in Australia and New Zealand
    d. 2019 World Cup in England and Wales

20. What was the first Test match to be affected by a terrorist attack?

    a. Pakistan vs. Sri Lanka, Lahore, 2009
    b. India vs. Pakistan, Karachi, 2004
    c. South Africa vs. Sri Lanka, Colombo, 1998
    d. New Zealand vs. Pakistan, Karachi, 2002

21. Which Test saw England winning after following on, famously known as "Botham's Ashes"?

    a. England vs. Australia, Headingley, 1981
    b. England vs. Australia, Edgbaston, 2005

c. England vs. Australia, The Oval, 2009
  d. England vs. Australia, Trent Bridge, 2015

22. What significant event occurred during the 2003 World Cup match between Zimbabwe and Namibia?
    a. The match set the record for the most extras in a World Cup game.
    b. It was the shortest completed match in World Cup history.
    c. Political protests took place during the match.
    d. It was the last international match for both team's captains.

23. Which match is celebrated for Viv Richards' fastest Test century by balls faced?
    a. West Indies vs. England, Antigua, 1986
    b. West Indies vs. Australia, Barbados, 1984
    c. West Indies vs. India, Delhi, 1987
    d. West Indies vs. South Africa, Johannesburg, 1992

24. What was the result of the first-ever pink ball Test match?
    a. Draw
    b. Australia won
    c. New Zealand won
    d. South Africa won

25. Who hit six sixes in an over in a World Cup match?
    a. Yuvraj Singh
    b. Herschelle Gibbs
    c. Chris Gayle
    d. AB de Villiers

Quiz Answers

1. **B – Australia vs. West Indies, 1960, Brisbane.** Known as the "Greatest Test Match of the 20th Century," it was the first-ever Test match to end in a tie.
2. **A – India vs. Pakistan, Delhi, 1999.** Anil Kumble famously took all ten wickets in an innings during this match against Pakistan in Delhi.
3. **C – 438 by South Africa vs. Australia, 2008.** Achieved during the first Test at the WACA Ground in Perth, this record-breaking chase remains a testament to South Africa's resilience and batting depth, marking one of the most memorable moments in cricket history.
4. **C – 2019, England vs. New Zealand.** The 2019 World Cup final between England and New Zealand was decided by a Super Over after a tie in the regular match.
5. **A – West Indies vs. England, Antigua, 2004.** Brian Lara scored his record-breaking 400 not out in this match, the highest individual score in Test cricket.
6. **A – Carlos Brathwaite.** While Marlon Samuels was instrumental in setting up a strong position for the West Indies with his top-scoring innings in the 2016 T20 World Cup Final, it was Carlos Brathwaite who hit the actual winning runs. In the dramatic climax of the match, Brathwaite famously smashed four consecutive sixes off Ben Stokes in the final over to seal the victory, directly contributing to the West Indies' triumph over England.
7. **A – 1992 World Cup Semi-final vs. England.** In this infamous match, South Africa needed 22 runs from 1 ball after a rain rule miscalculation.
8. **A – Australia vs. West Indies, Brisbane, 1960.** This match was the first-ever tied Test in the history of cricket.
9. **C – 125 by Zimbabwe vs. Australia.** This remarkable defensive effort occurred during the 1983 World Cup, where Zimbabwe, in their debut World Cup match, managed to defend this small

total, securing a historic victory against a strong Australian team.
10. **B – Joginder Sharma.** Joginder Sharma bowled the final over in the 2007 World T20 final, where India clinched the title against Pakistan.
11. **B – Sri Lanka vs. India, 1997.** The Test match between Sri Lanka and India in 1997 saw the highest number of runs scored in a single game, with Sri Lanka amassing 952/6 declared.
12. **A – Kevin O'Brien.** Kevin O'Brien holds the record for the fastest century in World Cup history, scoring 100 runs from just 50 balls for Ireland against England in 2011.
13. **A – Australia vs. England, Old Trafford, 1993.** This match was notable for Shane Warne's "Ball of the Century" to Mike Gatting.
14. **B – South Africa vs. Australia, Johannesburg, 2006** (This match holds the record for the highest scoring ODI ever played, where South Africa successfully chased down Australia's total of 434.
15. **A – Kumar Sangakkara and Mahela Jayawardene vs. South Africa, Colombo, 2006.** They set the highest ever Test partnership of 624 runs against South Africa.
16. **C – 2007 vs. Sri Lanka.** Australia won the 2007 World Cup final against Sri Lanka by 53 runs (D/L method), one of the largest margins by runs.
17. **A – Belinda Clark.** Belinda Clark scored a double century in a Women's ODI World Cup, becoming the first player to achieve this milestone.
18. **C – It was the first-ever Test match to end in a tie.** The 1960 tied Test match between Australia and West Indies was historic as it was the first Test match ever to end in a tie.
19. **B – 2011 World Cup in India, Sri Lanka, and Bangladesh.** Ireland defeated England in a dramatic match during the 2011 World Cup, marking one of the biggest upsets.
20. **A – Pakistan vs. Sri Lanka, Lahore, 2009.** This Test match was notably affected by a terrorist attack, targeting the Sri Lankan team bus in Lahore.

21. **A – England vs. Australia, Headingley, 1981.** Known as "Botham's Ashes," this Test saw England winning after following on, with Ian Botham playing a pivotal role.
22. **C – Political protests took place during the match.** During the 2003 World Cup match between Zimbabwe and Namibia, political protests over the situation in Zimbabwe were a significant event.
23. **A – West Indies vs. England, Antigua, 1986.** Viv Richards set a record for the fastest Test century by balls faced in this match.
24. **B – Australia won.** Australia won the first-ever pink ball Test match, played against New Zealand in Adelaide, 2015.
25. **B – Herschelle Gibbs.** Herschelle Gibbs hit six sixes in an over in a World Cup match, achieving this feat in the 2007 World Cup against the Netherlands.

Did You Know?

1. The first tied Test between Australia and the West Indies in 1960 led to a standing ovation from the crowd, a rare moment in cricket history.
2. The 1956 Test match between England and Australia featured Jim Laker taking a record 19 wickets in a single match, a feat unmatched to this day.
3. In the 1983 World Cup final, India defeated the West Indies against all odds, marking the first time a team outside the traditional powerhouses won the World Cup.
4. Sachin Tendulkar scored his 100th international century against Bangladesh in the Asia Cup 2012, a milestone no other player has reached.
5. In the 2001 Kolkata Test against Australia, India became only the third team in history to win a Test match after following on.
6. The 1992 World Cup final at the Melbourne Cricket Ground saw a record crowd of over 87,000 spectators, the highest ever for a cricket final at the time.
7. The Timeless Test between England and South Africa in 1939 lasted for 10 days, only to end in a draw because the English team needed to catch their ship home.

8. Kenya's stunning victory over Sri Lanka in the 2003 World Cup is one of the biggest upsets in cricket history, showcasing the unpredictable nature of the sport.
9. On debut, England's Graham Gooch faced the first ball of the 1975 World Cup and scored the tournament's first ever century.
10. The 1992 World Cup semi-final between England and South Africa ended controversially with South Africa needing an impossible 22 runs from one ball after a rain interruption recalculated the target.
11. In the 2007 World T20, Yuvraj Singh hit the fastest fifty in T20 internationals off just 12 balls against England, which included six sixes in an over off Stuart Broad.
12. Sri Lanka's win in the 1996 World Cup is considered one of the most dramatic underdog stories in cricket history, as they defeated the much-favored Australia in the final.
13. The first-ever day/night Test match was played in November 2015 between Australia and New Zealand at the Adelaide Oval, introducing the pink ball to Test cricket.
14. Cricket was included in the 1900 Paris Olympics where only two teams competed, Great Britain and France, with Great Britain winning the gold medal.
15. The 2019 World Cup final is the only instance in the history of cricket where a World Cup final was decided by a Super Over after the match tied, and the Super Over itself also ended in a tie.

CHAPTER 8:
INNOVATIONS IN CRICKET (T20, THE HUNDRED)

1. What year was the first official Twenty20 (T20) international match played?

    a. 2003
    b. 2005
    c. 2007
    d. 2001

2. Which team won the first ICC T20 World Cup?

    a. India
    b. Australia
    c. England
    d. West Indies

3. What is the maximum number of overs per bowler in a standard T20 match?

    a. 4
    b. 5
    c. 6
    d. 3

4. The Hundred is a cricket format introduced by which country?

    a. Australia
    b. India
    c. England
    d. South Africa

5. How many balls are bowled in a single innings of The Hundred?
   a. 100
   b. 120
   c. 80
   d. 50

6. Who was the first player to score a century in The Hundred?
   a. Liam Livingstone
   b. Jonny Bairstow
   c. Joe Root
   d. Ben Stokes

7. In T20 cricket, what is the term used for a match that is reduced to 5 overs per side due to weather or other interruptions?
   a. Super Over
   b. Cut-throat
   c. Sprint Match
   d. 5-5 Cricket

8. Which bowler holds the record for the best bowling figures in a T20 international match?
   a. Lasith Malinga
   b. Ajantha Mendis
   c. Rashid Khan
   d. Shane Watson

9. What is the record for the highest individual score in a T20 international match?
   a. 156
   b. 172
   c. 145
   d. 162

10. Who hit six sixes in an over during a T20 international?
    a. Yuvraj Singh
    b. Chris Gayle
    c. Kieron Pollard
    d. Herschelle Gibbs

11. What year did The Hundred competition officially start?
    a. 2020
    b. 2021
    c. 2019
    d. 2018

12. Which city's team won the inaugural season of The Hundred?
    a. Manchester
    b. Birmingham
    c. London
    d. Leeds

13. What is the unique feature of The Hundred concerning bowler's deliveries?
    a. Bowlers can deliver either 5 or 10 consecutive balls.
    b. Bowlers can only bowl spin.
    c. Bowlers must switch ends after every 10 balls.
    d. No bowler can bowl more than 20 balls per game.

14. Who holds the record for the fastest fifty in T20 internationals?
    a. KL Rahul
    b. David Warner
    c. Colin Munro
    d. Yuvraj Singh

15. In T20 cricket, what happens if the fielding team doesn't start the last over within the allotted 75 minutes?
    a. The batting team is awarded extra runs.
    b. The fielding team must remove one fielder outside the circle.
    c. The game is forfeited.
    d. The captain is fined.

16. What unique rule is applied to bowlers in The Hundred?
    a. Bowlers can bowl from either end at will.
    b. A bowler can deliver two consecutive overs.
    c. A bowler can switch bowling hands mid-over.
    d. None of the above.

17. What was the highest team score in a T20 World Cup match?

    a. 260
    b. 248
    c. 230
    d. 241

18. Which country hosted the inaugural T20 World Cup?

    a. India
    b. South Africa
    c. England
    d. Australia

19. Which team scored the lowest total in a T20 World Cup match?

    a. Canada
    b. Netherlands
    c. Kenya
    d. Bermuda

20. In T20 cricket, what is the penalty for a no-ball?

    a. 1 run
    b. 2 runs
    c. Free hit
    d. Both b and c

21. Who was the first captain to win the T20 World Cup?

    a. MS Dhoni
    b. Michael Clarke
    c. Darren Sammy
    d. Paul Collingwood

22. How many teams competed in the first season of The Hundred?

    a. 6
    b. 8
    c. 10
    d. 12

23. Which player has hit the most sixes in a single T20 World Cup tournament?

a. Chris Gayle
   b. Brendon McCullum
   c. AB de Villiers
   d. Eoin Morgan

24. What record did Afghanistan set in a T20 International match?
    a. Highest team score
    b. Most sixes in an innings
    c. Fastest team hundred
    d. All of the above

25. Who scored the first century in a T20 World Cup match?
    a. Chris Gayle
    b. Brendon McCullum
    c. Kevin Pietersen
    d. Mahela Jayawardene

Quiz Answers

1. **B – 2005.** The first official Twenty20 international match was played in 2005.
2. **A – India.** India won the first ICC T20 World Cup in 2007.
3. **A – 4.** In a standard T20 match, the maximum number of overs per bowler is 4.
4. **C – England.** The Hundred is a cricket format introduced by England.
5. **A – 100.** In The Hundred, 100 balls are bowled in a single innings.
6. **A – Liam Livingstone.** Liam Livingstone was the first player to score a century in The Hundred.
7. **D – 5-5 Cricket.** In T20 cricket, a match reduced to 5 overs per side due to interruptions is often referred to as 5-5 cricket.
8. **B – Ajantha Mendis.** Ajantha Mendis holds the record for the best bowling figures in a T20 international match.
9. **B – 172.** The record for the highest individual score in a T20 international match is 172.
10. **A – Yuvraj Singh.** Yuvraj Singh hit six sixes in an over during a T20 international match.
11. **B – 2021.** The Hundred competition officially started in 2021.
12. **C – London.** A London-based team won the inaugural season of The Hundred.
13. **A – Bowlers can deliver either 5 or 10 consecutive balls.** In The Hundred, bowlers have the option to deliver either 5 or 10 consecutive balls.
14. **D – Yuvraj Singh.** Yuvraj Singh holds the record for the fastest fifty in T20 internationals.
15. **B – The fielding team must remove one fielder outside the circle.** If the fielding team doesn't start the last over within 75 minutes in T20 cricket, they must remove one fielder outside the circle.
16. **B – A bowler can deliver two consecutive overs.** In The Hundred, a bowler can deliver two consecutive overs.
17. **A – 260.** The highest team score in a T20 World Cup match is 260.

18. **B – South Africa.** South Africa hosted the inaugural T20 World Cup.
19. **D – Netherlands.** The Netherlands scored the lowest total in a T20 World Cup match.
20. **D – Both b and c.** The penalty for a no-ball in T20 cricket includes 2 runs and a free hit.
21. **A – MS Dhoni.** MS Dhoni was the first captain to win the T20 World Cup.
22. **B – 8.** Eight teams competed in the first season of The Hundred.
23. **A – Chris Gayle.** Chris Gayle has hit the most sixes in a single T20 World Cup tournament.
24. **D – All of the above.** Afghanistan set multiple records in T20 International matches, including the highest team score, most sixes in an innings, and the fastest team hundred.
25. **A – Chris Gayle.** Chris Gayle scored the first century in a T20 World Cup match.

Did You Know?

1. T20 cricket was formally introduced by the England and Wales Cricket Board (ECB) in 2003 as a way to make cricket more appealing to younger audiences and to fit the game into shorter, more dynamic formats.
2. The first international T20 match was played between Australia and New Zealand in 2005, and players wore 1980s retro kits as a promotional gimmick.
3. The Hundred introduced several unique rules, including a change of ends after 10 balls and strategic timeouts that can be called by the fielding team.
4. Inspired by the success of the Indian Premier League (IPL), T20 leagues sprang up all over the world, including the Big Bash League in Australia and the Caribbean Premier League.
5. The Hundred was the first professional cricket competition to use a 'Golden Over' — a concept where a set number of balls can score double runs.

6. The Hundred was also the first major UK sports competition to launch with a sustainability plan, aiming to set new standards in environmental responsibility.
7. Tymal Mills bowled the fastest ball in the inaugural season of The Hundred, clocking in at 93.3 mph (150.2 km/h).
8. The Hundred was the first cricket event to extensively integrate live data and analytics into the broadcast, providing real-time insights into player performance and game dynamics.
9. The IPL and other T20 leagues have seen significant investments and appearances from global celebrities, enhancing the glamour and appeal of the matches.
10. The fastest fifty in T20 international cricket was scored in just 12 balls, highlighting the explosive batting style that T20 cricket encourages.
11. T20 cricket has been credited with significantly increasing participation rates among younger players globally due to its exciting and accessible format.
12. The T20 World Cup in 2014 was the first international tournament to use LED bails and stumps, which light up when dislodged.
13. T20 cricket has been a major factor in the rising popularity and professionalization of women's cricket, evidenced by increasing attendance and viewing figures for women's T20 matches.
14. The Hundred has seen teams employ advanced analytics and artificial intelligence in selecting teams and strategizing, a trend that is increasingly influencing how cricket is played and coached.

CHAPTER 9:
THE EVOLUTION OF CRICKET EQUIPMENT

1. What was the traditional shape of early cricket bats before evolving to their current flat form?
   a. a. Round like a hockey stick
   b. b. Triangular
   c. c. Rectangular
   d. d. Oval

2. When did protective helmets become commonplace in cricket?
   a. 1950s
   b. 1970s
   c. 1980s
   d. 1990s

3. Which company pioneered the introduction of carbon-fiber reinforcement in cricket bat spines to enhance performance and durability?
   a. Gray-Nicolls
   b. Kookaburra
   c. Gunn & Moore
   d. MRF

4. In what year did the International Cricket Council (ICC) standardize the dimensions of a cricket bat?
   a. 1774
   b. 1835

    c. 1979
    d. 2001

5. What innovation in cricket bats occurred in the 1970s?

    a. Aluminum bats
    b. Fiberglass covering
    c. Carbon fiber handles
    d. Synthetic rubber grips

6. Who is known for popularizing the modern thigh pad in cricket?

    a. Sunil Gavaskar
    b. Viv Richards
    c. Clive Lloyd
    d. Dennis Lillee

7. What significant change did Kerry Packer's World Series Cricket bring to cricket equipment?

    a. Colored clothing
    b. Protective helmets
    c. White cricket balls
    d. Both a and c

8. When were colored cricket uniforms first introduced?

    a. 1977
    b. 1982
    c. 1992
    d. 2001

9. What was the main reason for the introduction of the white cricket ball?

    a. Better visibility under lights
    b. Aesthetic appeal
    c. Durability
    d. Less wear and tear

10. Which innovation in cricket pads increased mobility for batsmen?

a. Lighter foam materials
b. Knee roll adjustments
c. Velcro straps
d. High-density sponge

11. In which year were stump cameras first widely recognized and used extensively in international cricket broadcasts?

    a. a. 1992
    b. b. 1983
    c. c. 1996
    d. d. 1988

12. How did the use of aluminum bats impact the game before being banned?

    a. Increased bat speed
    b. Louder sound
    c. Increased durability
    d. Altered ball behavior

13. What is the primary material used in manufacturing cricket balls today?

    a. Rubber
    b. Leather
    c. Synthetic fiber
    d. Plastic

14. Which development in cricket helmets improved player comfort?

    a. Ventilation systems
    b. Adjustable chin straps
    c. Padded interiors
    d. All of the above

15. When did the ICC officially prohibit the use of aluminum bats in matches?

    a. 1975
    b. 1979
    c. 1981
    d. 1985

16. What was the purpose of introducing high-visibility, fluorescent sightscreens?
    a. To assist batsmen under twilight conditions
    b. To attract younger audiences
    c. To improve the aesthetic of stadiums
    d. To increase sponsorship visibility

17. Which innovation was first seen in cricket spikes to improve grip on the pitch?
    a. Rubber soles
    b. Metal spikes
    c. Interchangeable studs
    d. Synthetic materials

18. Which of the following enhancements were introduced to cricket gloves in the 1980s to increase player protection?
    a. Extra padding on the backhand
    b. Fiberglass inserts
    c. Hardened plastic shells
    d. All of the above

19. Who was responsible for the introduction of lightweight foam batting pads?
    a. Duncan Fearnley
    b. Ian Botham
    c. Sachin Tendulkar
    d. Allan Border

20. What technology has been incorporated into cricket stumps to help in close decisions?
    a. LED bails
    b. Microchips
    c. Pressure sensors
    d. HD cameras

21. How has the cricket bat handle evolved to reduce shock impact?
    a. Use of rubber grips
    b. Introduction of cane and rubber inserts

c. Switch to synthetic materials
   d. Carbon fiber reinforcement

22. When was the first recorded use of shin guards in cricket?
    a. Early 1900s
    b. 1930s
    c. 1950s
    d. 1970s

23. What type of ball was used during the first-ever day/night Test match?
    a. Traditional red ball
    b. White ball
    c. Pink ball
    d. Orange ball

24. What innovation was introduced to cricket shoes in the late 1990s to improve performance?
    a. Lighter materials
    b. Water-resistant uppers
    c. Aerodynamic design
    d. Enhanced arch support

25. When did the practice of covering cricket pitches to protect them from rain begin?
    a. 1864
    b. 1880
    c. 1901
    d. 1920

Quiz Answers

1. **A – Round like a hockey stick.** Early cricket bats were shaped more like hockey sticks, designed to hit a ball that was rolled along the ground.
2. **C – 1980s.** Protective helmets became commonplace in cricket during the 1980s, largely due to increased bowling speeds and safety concerns.
3. **B – Kookaburra.** They were among the first to introduce enhancements in cricket bats, including the use of carbon-fiber reinforced spines. This advancement aimed to improve the durability and performance of cricket bats, leveraging modern materials to enhance traditional equipment.
4. **C – 1979.** The International Cricket Council (ICC) standardized the dimensions of a cricket bat in 1979.
5. **B – Fiberglass covering.** In the 1970s, fiberglass coverings were introduced to cricket bats to increase durability and protect the wood from wear.
6. **A – Sunil Gavaskar.** Sunil Gavaskar is known for popularizing the modern thigh pad in cricket, particularly after facing fast bowlers without adequate protection earlier in his career.
7. **D – Both a and c.** Kerry Packer's World Series Cricket introduced significant changes like colored clothing and white cricket balls, enhancing the game's visual appeal and suiting television broadcasts.
8. **A – 1977.** Colored cricket uniforms were first introduced in 1977 as part of Kerry Packer's World Series Cricket.
9. **A – Better visibility under lights.** The white cricket ball was introduced for better visibility under artificial lights during night matches.
10. **A – Lighter foam materials.** Innovation in cricket pads included the use of lighter foam materials, which increased mobility for batsmen while maintaining protection.
11. **A – 1992.** Stump cameras were first extensively used during the 1992 Cricket World Cup, which marked a significant advancement in cricket broadcasting technology. This innovation provided viewers with unique and close-up views

of the cricketing action, particularly around the wickets, enhancing the overall viewing experience.
12. **D – Altered ball behavior.** Aluminum bats were briefly used but were banned because they altered the ball's behavior upon impact, potentially giving batsmen an unfair advantage.
13. **B – Leather.** Cricket balls are primarily made from leather, which encases a core traditionally made from cork and string.
14. **D – All of the above.** Developments in cricket helmets have included ventilation systems, adjustable chin straps, and padded interiors to improve player comfort and safety.
15. **B – 1979.** The ICC officially prohibited the use of aluminum bats in matches starting in 1979, following controversy over their use.
16. **A – To assist batsmen under twilight conditions.** High-visibility, fluorescent sightscreens were introduced to assist batsmen in seeing the ball better under varying light conditions, particularly during twilight.
17. **B – Metal spikes.** Metal spikes were one of the first innovations in cricket spikes to improve grip on the pitch, especially useful in wet conditions.
18. **D – All of the above.** In the 1980s, cricket gloves underwent several significant enhancements to increase player protection. These improvements included the addition of extra padding on the backhand, which provided better cushioning against fast deliveries. Additionally, fiberglass inserts were introduced, offering increased resistance to impact and helping to distribute the force more evenly across the glove. Hardened plastic shells were also incorporated into the glove design, greatly enhancing the protection by providing a tougher barrier against high-speed balls. Each of these developments played a crucial role in improving safety standards for batsmen, addressing the challenges posed by the evolving pace and intensity of the game.
19. **A – Duncan Fearnley.** Duncan Fearnley was responsible for the introduction of lightweight foam batting pads, which provided better mobility and comfort for batsmen.

20. **A – LED bails.** LED bails have been incorporated into cricket stumps to help in close decisions, lighting up when dislodged to clearly indicate a wicket.
21. **B – Introduction of cane and rubber inserts.** Cricket bat handles evolved to include cane and rubber inserts to reduce shock impact, providing better grip and comfort for the batsman.
22. **A – Early 1900s.** The first recorded use of shin guards in cricket occurred in the early 1900s, providing lower leg protection for batsmen and close fielders.
23. **C – Pink ball.** The pink ball was used during the first-ever day/night Test match to provide better visibility under floodlights compared to the traditional red ball.
24. **A – Lighter materials.** In the late 1990s, cricket shoes saw the introduction of lighter materials, significantly reducing the weight of the shoes to improve players' agility and speed.
25. **B – 1880.** The practice of covering cricket pitches to protect them from rain began in 1880, helping to preserve the playing surface during wet weather and ensuring more consistent playing conditions.

Did You Know?

1. The first cricket balls used in the 16th century were made from a core of rags or wool, which provided very inconsistent bounce and flight.
2. Originally, cricket bats resembled hockey sticks to cope with the rolling technique of bowling used in the early days of the sport.
3. The first cricket pads were made from cork and were initially used only by batsmen to protect themselves from underarm bowling.
4. Cricket shoes evolved from normal leather boots to boots with spikes in the early 19th century to provide players with better grip on the field.
5. The modern cricket helmet was not introduced until the late 1970s. Before then, batsmen wore caps or nothing at all, even facing fast bowlers.

6. The first use of colored clothing in cricket was during Kerry Packer's World Series Cricket in the late 1970s, a major shift from traditional white.
7. The jockstrap, an essential piece of protective equipment, was introduced into cricket in the 1870s to protect players from severe injuries.
8. Early wicket-keeping gloves were merely padded leather gloves, quite similar to those used in gardening. Modern versions are highly specialized with webbing between the fingers.
9. Dennis Lillee famously used an aluminum bat in a Test match in 1979, but it was quickly banned by the ICC for damaging the leather ball.
10. The introduction of the third umpire in 1992 was facilitated by the use of video technology, a significant shift from solely on-field decisions.
11. First introduced in the 1990s, stump cameras and microphones added a new dimension to broadcast cricket, allowing audiences to catch the close action and on-field communications.
12. The introduction of white balls and colored clothing revolutionized cricket, making it possible to play the sport under floodlights and increasing its global appeal.
13. In the early 2000s, manufacturers experimented with reinforcing cricket bats with graphite to enhance performance, although this was later banned to preserve the traditional nature of the equipment.
14. Systems like Hawk-Eye, first introduced in 2001, use cameras to track the trajectory of the ball, aiding umpires with LBW decisions and changing how the game is viewed.
15. To protect the willow and extend the bat's lifespan, players began using anti-scuff coverings on their bats in the late 20th century, a practice that has now become common.

CHAPTER 10:

CONTROVERSIES AND SCANDALS

1. Which cricketer was involved in a controversy for tampering with the ball using a mint during a match in 2016?

   a. Steve Smith
   b. Faf du Plessis
   c. David Warner
   d. Virat Kohli

2. In which year was the Indian Premier League (IPL) spot-fixing scandal uncovered?

   a. 2010
   b. 2012
   c. 2013
   d. 2015

3. Which Pakistan cricketer received a five-year ban for spot-fixing in 2010?

   a. Mohammad Asif
   b. Salman Butt
   c. Mohammad Amir
   d. All of the above

4. What was the name of the bookmaker involved in the 2000 match-fixing scandal?

   a. Sanjeev Chawla
   b. Mukesh Gupta
   c. Manoj Prabhakar
   d. Hansie Cronje

5. Which Australian cricketer received a ban in 2003 for a doping violation?
   a. Shane Warne
   b. Ricky Ponting
   c. Glenn McGrath
   d. Mark Waugh

6. What was the reason behind Shane Warne and Mark Waugh receiving fines in 1994?
   a. Match-fixing
   b. Doping
   c. Providing pitch and weather information to bookmakers
   d. Public misconduct

7. What triggered the 2010 Pakistani cricket tour of England controversy, widely known as the 'spot-fixing' scandal?
   a. Players betting on matches
   b. Unauthorized use of communication devices during play
   c. Deliberate no-balls for monetary gain
   d. Disagreements over team selection policies

8. In the 2008 Sydney Test, which country was involved in a controversial umpiring decision against India?
   a. Australia
   b. South Africa
   c. England
   d. New Zealand

9. What was the controversial tactic used by England's bowlers in the 1932-33 Ashes series?
   a. Reverse swing
   b. Bodyline bowling
   c. Doosra
   d. Switch hit

10. Which South African captain confessed to match-fixing in 2000?
    a. Graeme Smith
    b. Hansie Cronje

- c. AB de Villiers
- d. Faf du Plessis

11. Which Sri Lankan cricketer was charged by the ICC in 2018 for failing to cooperate with an anti-corruption investigation?
    - a. Kumar Sangakkara
    - b. Angelo Mathews
    - c. Sanath Jayasuriya
    - d. Tillakaratne Dilshan

12. Which team was controversially bowled out for 26 runs, the lowest ever Test score, in 1955?
    - a. India
    - b. New Zealand
    - c. South Africa
    - d. England

13. What action did Trevor Chappell take in the 1981 underarm bowling incident?
    - a. Bowled an underarm delivery on the final ball
    - b. Refused to bowl the final over
    - c. Walked off the field in protest
    - d. Apologized publicly after the match

14. What was unusual about Sunil Gavaskar's reaction during the 1981 Melbourne Test?
    - a. He walked off the field after being given out
    - b. He refused to leave the crease after being dismissed
    - c. He batted left-handed
    - d. He bowled underarm

15. Who was implicated in the 2018 ball-tampering scandal in South Africa?
    - a. Steve Smith, David Warner, and Cameron Bancroft
    - b. Aaron Finch, Mitchell Starc, and Pat Cummins
    - c. Tim Paine, Nathan Lyon, and Josh Hazlewood
    - d. Adam Zampa, Glenn Maxwell, and James Faulkner

16. What was the result of the "Big Three" controversy in ICC management?
    a. Redistribution of ICC funds
    b. Increased power for India, Australia, and England
    c. Division among ICC members
    d. All of the above

17. Which West Indies player is celebrated for his act of sportsmanship in not running out Pakistan's batsman during a critical moment of the 1987 World Cup?
    a. Brian Lara
    b. Viv Richards
    c. Courtney Walsh
    d. Michael Holding

18. What was a significant concern for international cricket teams touring Pakistan during the early 2000s?
    a. Pitch tampering
    b. Poor accommodations
    c. Security concerns
    d. Unfair team selection

19. Which New Zealand cricketer confessed to match-fixing in 2014?
    a. Daniel Vettori
    b. Lou Vincent
    c. Brendon McCullum
    d. Ross Taylor

20. What caused the controversy during the 2006 Oval Test between England and Pakistan?
    a. Pakistan forfeited the match
    b. England refused to play
    c. Fans invaded the pitch
    d. It rained excessively

21. What was unusual about the coin toss in the 2011 World Cup semi-final between India and Sri Lanka?

a. It was done twice
b. The coin was lost
c. It was done in private
d. No coin was used

22. Which bowler was no-balled multiple times for throwing in Australia in 1995?

    a. Brett Lee
    b. Muttiah Muralitharan
    c. Shoaib Akhtar
    d. Shaun Tait

23. Which cricket board was suspended by the ICC in 2019 due to government interference?

    a. Zimbabwe
    b. Ireland
    c. Afghanistan
    d. Bangladesh

24. In what situation did Greg Chappell instruct his brother Trevor Chappell to bowl underarm in a one-day match against New Zealand?

    a. Last ball with three runs to win
    b. First ball of the last over
    c. Last ball with six runs to win
    d. During the middle of the innings as a tactical ploy

25. What was the outcome of the "Sandpapergate" scandal for Australian cricket?

    a. Leadership changes
    b. Long-term suspensions for key players
    c. A complete overhaul of the national team coaching staff
    d. All of the above

Quiz Answers

1. **B – Faf du Plessis.** Faf du Plessis was involved in a ball-tampering controversy during a match in 2016 where he was found using a mint to alter the condition of the ball.
2. **C – 2013.** The Indian Premier League (IPL) spot-fixing scandal was uncovered in 2013, involving allegations of betting and match-fixing.
3. **D – All of the above.** Mohammad Asif, Salman Butt, and Mohammad Amir all received bans in 2010 for their involvement in spot-fixing during a Test match against England.
4. **A – Sanjeev Chawla.** Sanjeev Chawla was a key bookmaker involved in the 2000 cricket match-fixing scandal that implicated several cricketers, including South African captain Hansie Cronje.
5. **A – Shane Warne.** In 2003, Shane Warne was suspended for one year after testing positive for a banned diuretic. Warne claimed the substance was in a weight loss pill given to him by his mother. This incident, while significant, did not result in a life ban but did notably impact Warne's illustrious cricketing career.
6. **C – Providing pitch and weather information to bookmakers.** In 1994, Shane Warne and Mark Waugh were fined for providing pitch and weather information to a bookmaker.
7. **C – Deliberate no-balls for monetary gain.** The 2010 Pakistani cricket tour of England controversy, often referred to as the 'spot-fixing' scandal, involved several Pakistani players who were found guilty of deliberately bowling no-balls at specific times during the Test match at Lord's. This was orchestrated as part of a spot-fixing arrangement with a bookmaker, who had paid the players to perform these specific actions at predetermined times. The scandal was uncovered through a sting operation by a news outlet, leading to significant repercussions for the involved players, including bans and legal actions.

8. **A – Australia.** In the 2008 Sydney Test, a controversial umpiring decision went against India, involving several contentious moments during the match.
9. **B – Bodyline bowling.** The controversial tactic used by England's bowlers in the 1932-33 Ashes series was known as Bodyline bowling, involving fast, short-pitched deliveries aimed at the batsmen's bodies.
10. **B – Hansie Cronje.** South African captain Hansie Cronje confessed to match-fixing in 2000, shocking the cricket world.
11. **C – Sanath Jayasuriya.** In 2018, Sanath Jayasuriya, the former Sri Lankan cricket captain and a legendary cricketer, was charged by the International Cricket Council (ICC) for failing to cooperate with an anti-corruption investigation. The charges were not for direct involvement in match-fixing but were related to his non-cooperation with the ICC's efforts to investigate potential corrupt activities within cricket.
12. **B – New Zealand.** New Zealand was controversially bowled out for 26 runs against England in 1955, marking the lowest ever Test score.
13. **A – Bowled an underarm delivery on the final ball.** Trevor Chappell bowled an underarm delivery on the final ball of a match in 1981, instructed by his brother Greg Chappell, in a one-day international against New Zealand.
14. **A – He walked off the field after being given out.** Sunil Gavaskar's unusual reaction during the 1981 Melbourne Test involved him walking off the field after being controversially given out, though he was persuaded to return.
15. **A – Steve Smith, David Warner, and Cameron Bancroft.** In the 2018 ball-tampering scandal, known as "Sandpapergate," in South Africa, Steve Smith, David Warner, and Cameron Bancroft were implicated and faced significant suspensions.
16. **D – All of the above.** The "Big Three" controversy in ICC management led to the redistribution of ICC funds, increased power for India, Australia, and England, and division among ICC members.
17. **C – Courtney Walsh.** During the final moments of a crucial game, Walsh had the opportunity to run out Pakistan's Saleem

Jaffar, who was out of his crease before the ball was bowled. Instead of taking advantage of Jaffar's mistake, Walsh chose not to dismiss him, warning him instead.

18. **C – Security concerns.** During the early 2000s, security concerns due to regional instability significantly impacted international cricket teams' willingness to tour Pakistan, affecting the scheduling and location of numerous matches.
19. **B – Lou Vincent.** Lou Vincent, a New Zealand cricketer, confessed to match-fixing in 2014 and was subsequently banned for life.
20. **A – Pakistan forfeited the match.** The controversy during the 2006 Oval Test between England and Pakistan involved Pakistan forfeiting the match after being penalized for ball tampering.
21. **A – Done twice.** The coin toss in the 2011 World Cup semi-final between India and Sri Lanka was controversially done twice due to confusion about the call.
22. **B – Muttiah Muralitharan.** Muttiah Muralitharan was no-balled multiple times for throwing during a match in Australia in 1995, leading to significant controversy and discussions on bowling actions.
23. **A – Zimbabwe.** In 2019, the International Cricket Council (ICC) suspended Zimbabwe Cricket due to government interference, which violated the ICC's requirement for free and democratic governance in cricket administrations.
24. **C – Last ball with six runs to win.** Greg Chappell instructed his brother Trevor Chappell to bowl underarm on the last ball of a one-day match against New Zealand when six runs were required to win, creating a significant uproar.
25. **D – All of the above.** The outcome of the "Sandpapergate" scandal for Australian cricket included leadership changes, long-term suspensions for key players, and a complete overhaul of the national team coaching staff.

Did You Know?

1. The first major controversy in international cricket occurred in 1877 when an Australian player was accused of punching an English player during the first-ever Test match.
2. In 1932, Douglas Jardine of England wore silk underwear to protect himself from bodyline bowling—a tactic his own team invented.
3. In 1958, West Indies fast bowler Roy Gilchrist was called for throwing, a rare accusation at the time, causing a major uproar during the series against England.
4. In the 1990s, players were accused of using sunscreen to tamper with the ball, making it swing unpredictably, though no formal charges were ever proven.
5. Sarfraz Nawaz of Pakistan is credited with discovering reverse swing in the late 1970s, a technique that later led to various ball-tampering scandals.
6. In 1981, Greg Chappell was the first captain to resign due to a controversy after instructing his brother to bowl underarm against New Zealand.
7. Kerry Packer's World Series Cricket in 1977 led to major reforms in the game, including player salaries and game formats, after initial severe criticism and controversy.
8. The first televised cricket match where allegations of fixing were made was during the 1992 World Cup, involving players from Pakistan.
9. In 1994, England's players were accused of using earpieces during a match against New Zealand, a method thought to be used for receiving coach instructions.
10. The use of colored wickets was briefly experimented with in the early 2000s but was discontinued after players and spectators complained about visibility issues.
11. Following the match-fixing scandals of the late 1990s, the ICC established its Anti-Corruption Unit in 2000 to combat corruption in cricket.

12. In 2003, Henry Olonga and Andy Flower wore black armbands during a World Cup match to protest against the "death of democracy" in Zimbabwe.
13. The first major controversy in women's cricket involved allegations of sexual discrimination against the Australian Women's Cricket Board in 1997.
14. The introduction of the Decision Review System (DRS) in 2008 led to heated debates and controversies regarding its accuracy and implementation.
15. In 2018, the MeToo movement reached cricket, with several female reporters and professionals coming forward with allegations of sexual harassment within the sport.

CHAPTER 11:

THE ROLE OF THE ECB

1. In which year was the ECB officially formed?
    a. 1963
    b. 1973
    c. 1997
    d. 2003

2. What was the ECB's predecessor organization called?
    a. British Cricket Board
    b. Test and County Cricket Board (TCCB)
    c. English Cricket Federation
    d. UK Cricket Association

3. What significant innovation did the ECB introduce in 2003?
    a. Powerplays in ODIs
    b. T20 cricket format
    c. Hawk-Eye technology
    d. Pink cricket balls

4. Which tournament is specifically organized by the ECB to enhance domestic cricket in England and Wales?
    a. The Ashes
    b. County Championship
    c. The Hundred
    d. NatWest T20 Blast

5. Who was the first female to be appointed to the ECB's board of directors?

a. Clare Connor
   b. Rachel Heyhoe Flint
   c. Charlotte Edwards
   d. Isa Guha

6. What is the ECB's initiative called that aims to increase participation in cricket across England and Wales?
   a. Cricket Unleashed
   b. Chance to Shine
   c. Play Cricket
   d. All Stars Cricket

7. In what year did the ECB take over the governance of women's cricket in England?
   a. 1998
   b. 2005
   c. 2009
   d. 2013

8. What program did the ECB launch to combat racism and promote diversity within cricket?
   a. Cricket Against Racism
   b. Respect in Sport
   c. Action for Equality
   d. Inspiring Generations

9. What controversy involved the ECB in 2014 related to a player's biography?
   a. Kevin Pietersen's autobiography release
   b. Andrew Flintoff's revelations about depression
   c. Michael Vaughan's criticism of selection policies
   d. Ian Botham's criticism of ECB management

10. Which groundbreaking competition did the ECB propose in 2019 to attract younger audiences to cricket?
    a. The Hundred
    b. T20 Blast
    c. Vitality Blast
    d. Super Smash

11. How does the ECB promote grassroots cricket?
    a. Sponsorship deals
    b. Funding local clubs
    c. Televising local matches
    d. Hosting annual awards
12. What was the main reason behind the creation of the T20 format by the ECB?
    a. To compete with football
    b. To boost declining cricket viewership
    c. To simplify the rules of cricket
    d. To create a shorter version of Test cricket
13. Which ECB initiative is specifically designed to introduce cricket to children aged 5 to 8 years old?
    a. All Stars Cricket
    b. Dynamos Cricket
    c. Kwik Cricket
    d. Junior Championships
14. What financial strategy did the ECB implement to deal with the impact of the COVID-19 pandemic?
    a. Salary cuts for players
    b. Austerity measures
    c. Fundraising matches
    d. Emergency loan scheme
15. Which award is given by the ECB to recognize outstanding young players?
    a. Young Cricketer of the Year
    b. Future Stars Award
    c. Emerging Talent Trophy
    d. Best Junior Player
16. How did the ECB contribute to international cricket development?
    a. Hosting ICC tournaments
    b. Training foreign coaches

c. Funding cricket in developing countries
   d. Promoting cricket diplomacy

17. What role does the ECB play in player disputes?
    a. Arbitration
    b. Legal advice
    c. Conflict resolution
    d. Contract negotiations

18. What was a significant action taken by the ECB during the 2005 Ashes concerning broadcasting rights?
    a. Moved from free-to-air television to a subscription service
    b. Launched its own streaming service
    c. Sold rights to the highest bidder
    d. Partnered with multiple broadcasters

19. How has the ECB addressed player mental health?
    a. Mandatory counseling sessions
    b. Mindfulness training
    c. Partnership with mental health organizations
    d. Creating a wellness app

20. What innovation in broadcasting did the ECB introduce for The Hundred?
    a. Virtual reality experiences
    b. Interactive live streams
    c. Ultra HD broadcasts
    d. Fan-controlled cameras

21. Which sustainability initiative is promoted by the ECB?
    a. Carbon-neutral stadiums
    b. Zero waste matches
    c. Green cricket initiatives
    d. All of the above

22. What historic decision did the ECB make regarding women's cricket salaries in 2020?
    a. Equal pay with men
    b. Minimum wage establishment

    c. Performance-based incentives
    d. Professional contracts

23. How does the ECB handle anti-doping?
    a. Regular testing
    b. Player education programs
    c. Strict penalties
    d. All of the above

24. What community program is supported by the ECB to help disadvantaged youth?
    a. Cricket for Change
    b. Hit for Six
    c. Street Cricket
    d. Bowl Out Poverty

25. What measures has the ECB implemented to adapt playing conditions in response to the changing climate?
    a. Introducing heat rules
    b. Scheduling more day/night matches
    c. Providing additional water breaks
    d. All of the above

Quiz Answers

1. **C – 1997.** The ECB was officially formed in 1997, succeeding the Test and County Cricket Board.
2. **B – Test and County Cricket Board (TCCB).** The predecessor organization to the ECB was the Test and County Cricket Board, which governed cricket in England and Wales before the ECB's formation.
3. **B – T20 cricket format.** In 2003, the ECB introduced the T20 cricket format as a way to revitalize interest in the sport, particularly among younger audiences.
4. **C – The Hundred.** The Hundred is a cricket tournament organized by the ECB, specifically designed to enhance domestic cricket in England and Wales with a new 100-ball format.
5. **A – Clare Connor.** Clare Connor was the first female to be appointed to the ECB's board of directors, marking a significant step towards gender equality in cricket administration.
6. **D – All Stars Cricket.** The All Stars Cricket initiative by the ECB aims to increase participation in cricket across England and Wales by engaging children in the sport from a young age.
7. **A – 1998**
8. **D – Inspiring Generations.** The ECB launched the "Inspiring Generations" program to combat racism and promote diversity within cricket.
9. **A – Kevin Pietersen's autobiography release.** In 2014, the ECB was involved in a controversy related to Kevin Pietersen's autobiography, which included critical revelations about the ECB and team dynamics.
10. **A – The Hundred.** In 2019, the ECB proposed The Hundred, a groundbreaking competition aimed at attracting younger audiences to cricket with a faster, more accessible format.
11. **B – Funding local clubs.** The ECB promotes grassroots cricket primarily by funding local clubs, helping to develop facilities and increase participation at the community level.
12. **B – To boost declining cricket viewership.** The main reason behind the creation of the T20 format by the ECB was to boost

declining viewership and bring an exciting, shorter format to attract new fans.
13. **A – All Stars Cricket.** All Stars Cricket is an ECB initiative launched to introduce children aged 5 to 8 years old to cricket, focusing on fun, inclusive activities that build fundamental movement skills.
14. **D – Emergency loan scheme.** During the COVID-19 pandemic, the ECB implemented an emergency loan scheme as part of its financial strategy to help support the cricket community through the crisis.
15. **A – Young Cricketer of the Year.** The "Young Cricketer of the Year" award is given by the ECB to recognize outstanding young players who have demonstrated exceptional talent and potential in the sport.
16. **A – Hosting ICC tournaments.** The ECB has contributed to international cricket development by hosting several ICC tournaments, thereby promoting the sport and facilitating its global growth.
17. **C – Conflict resolution.** The ECB plays a role in player disputes by offering conflict resolution services to help resolve issues that arise between players, teams, and other entities.
18. **A – Moved from free-to-air television to a subscription service.** In a significant shift during the 2005 Ashes, the ECB transferred broadcasting rights from free-to-air channels to Sky Sports, a subscription-based service, limiting free public access to live cricket broadcasts.
19. **C – Partnership with mental health organizations.** The ECB has addressed player mental health by forming partnerships with mental health organizations to provide support and resources for players.
20. **D – Fan-controlled cameras.** For The Hundred, the ECB introduced fan-controlled cameras, an innovative broadcasting feature that allowed viewers to select camera angles, enhancing interactivity and engagement during live matches.
21. **D – All of the above.** The ECB promotes several sustainability initiatives, including carbon-neutral stadiums, zero waste

matches, and green cricket initiatives, to reduce the environmental impact of cricket events.
22. **D – Professional contracts.** In 2020, the ECB made a historic decision regarding women's cricket salaries by offering professional contracts, significantly improving financial support for female cricketers.
23. **D – All of the above.** The ECB handles anti-doping through regular testing, player education programs, and strict penalties to maintain the integrity and fairness of the sport.
24. **A – Cricket for Change.** The ECB supports the "Cricket for Change" program, which helps disadvantaged youth by using cricket as a tool for positive social impact and personal development.
25. **D – All of the above.** In response to the changing climate, the ECB has implemented measures such as introducing heat rules, scheduling more day/night matches, and providing additional water breaks to ensure player safety and adapt playing conditions to increasingly variable weather patterns.

Did You Know?

1. The ECB introduced central contracts for England players in 2000, a significant reform that helped improve national team performance by managing players' workloads.
2. The ECB played a crucial role in the conceptualization and founding of the ICC Champions Trophy, initially known as the ICC KnockOut Tournament, in 1998.
3. In 2004, the ECB was among the first cricket boards to introduce a professional domestic Twenty20 competition, setting the stage for the global T20 boom.
4. The ECB's 'Cricket Unleashed' strategy, launched in 2016, aims to make cricket more accessible and engaging at all levels throughout England and Wales.
5. In 2019, the ECB launched an app for the England cricket team, providing fans with live scores, breaking news, and exclusive content.

6. The ECB's National Cricket Academy, established in 2003 at Loughborough University, has been a breeding ground for coaching innovations and elite player development.
7. The ECB has been a leader in promoting disability cricket, organizing national competitions for physically and visually impaired players.
8. In response to changing demographics, the ECB has developed targeted initiatives to increase cricket participation among British Asian communities.
9. The ECB has implemented 'The Spirit of Cricket' initiative in schools, promoting fair play and respect among young players.
10. Under the ECB's governance, the England women's cricket team won their first ICC Women's World Cup in 1973 and went on to secure multiple titles, including the famous 2017 World Cup win at home.
11. The ECB hosted the first day/night Test match in England in 2017, using a pink ball to attract more spectators and enhance the viewing experience.
12. The ECB has been at the forefront of addressing mental health issues in cricket, offering support programs and resources to players at all levels.
13. The ECB has established partnerships with various charities to use cricket as a tool for social change, including collaborations with the Lord's Taverners.
14. The ECB committed to the United Nations' Sports for Climate Action Framework in 2021, pledging to promote greater environmental responsibility in sports.
15. The ECB supports heritage projects that preserve and celebrate the history of cricket in England and Wales, including funding for cricket museums and historical archives.

CHAPTER 12:

WOMEN IN CRICKET

1. Who was the first woman to score a double century in a One Day International?

    a. Belinda Clark
    b. Mithali Raj
    c. Charlotte Edwards
    d. Meg Lanning

2. Which country won the first ICC Women's World Cup in 1973?

    a. Australia
    b. England
    c. New Zealand
    d. India

3. Who is the highest wicket-taker in Women's One Day Internationals?

    a. Jhulan Goswami
    b. Cathryn Fitzpatrick
    c. Ellyse Perry
    d. Anisa Mohammed

4. In what year did women's cricket debut at the Commonwealth Games?

    a. 1998
    b. 2002
    c. 2010
    d. 2022

5. Who was the first woman to be inducted into the ICC Cricket Hall of Fame?
   a. Rachael Heyhoe Flint
   b. Debbie Hockley
   c. Enid Bakewell
   d. Belinda Clark

6. What milestone did Mithali Raj achieve in Women's One Day Internationals?
   a. First woman to score 7,000 runs
   b. Highest individual score
   c. Most centuries
   d. Longest career span

7. Who holds the record for the best bowling figures in a Women's T20 International?
   a. Megan Schutt
   b. Poonam Yadav
   c. Anisa Mohammed
   d. Deepthi Sharma

8. Which team has won the most ICC Women's World Cup titles?
   a. Australia
   b. England
   c. India
   d. New Zealand

9. What significant barrier did Sarah Taylor break in English domestic cricket?
   a. First woman to play in a men's county cricket match
   b. First woman to captain a men's team
   c. First woman to coach a men's national team
   d. First woman to umpire in a men's international match

10. When was the Women's Big Bash League (WBBL) first introduced?
    a. 2013
    b. 2015

c. 2017
d. 2019

11. Who was the first woman to score a century in a Women's T20 International?

    a. Deandra Dottin
    b. Suzie Bates
    c. Harmanpreet Kaur
    d. Alyssa Healy

12. Which woman cricketer has won the ICC Women's Cricketer of the Year award the most times?

    a. Ellyse Perry
    b. Suzie Bates
    c. Mithali Raj
    d. Stafanie Taylor

13. In which year was the first Women's Cricket Super League held in England?

    a. 2014
    b. 2016
    c. 2018
    d. 2020

14. Who was the first woman cricketer to take 200 wickets in ODIs?

    a. Jhulan Goswami
    b. Cathryn Fitzpatrick
    c. Sian Ruck
    d. Isa Guha

15. Which female cricketer was named Wisden Leading Woman Cricketer in the World in 2017?

    a. Heather Knight
    b. Sarah Taylor
    c. Ellyse Perry
    d. Meg Lanning

16. What is the highest team score in Women's T20 internationals?

a. 216
   b. 221
   c. 232
   d. 250

17. Which of the following cricketers became captain of their national team at a notably young age?
    a. Mithali Raj
    b. Sana Mir
    c. Stafanie Taylor
    d. Sophie Devine

18. Which woman has umpired in the most international cricket matches?
    a. Kathy Cross
    b. Claire Polosak
    c. Sue Redfern
    d. Jacqueline Williams

19. What record did Amelia Kerr set in a Women's ODI?
    a. Highest individual score (232*)
    b. Most wickets in a match (7)
    c. Most runs in a series
    d. Fastest century

20. Who was the first female commentator in men's Test cricket?
    a. Isa Guha
    b. Anjum Chopra
    c. Lisa Sthalekar
    d. Melanie Jones

21. When did the ICC introduce a Women's Championship to determine qualification for the Women's World Cup?
    a. 2014
    b. 2016
    c. 2018
    d. 2020

22. Which woman has served as a coach in both women's and men's national cricket teams?

    a. Lisa Keightley
    b. Charlotte Edwards
    c. Clare Connor
    d. Julia Price

23. What was the first year that the Women's Asia Cup was held?

    a. 2004
    b. 2006
    c. 2008
    d. 2010

24. Which country hosted the first standalone ICC Women's T20 World Cup?

    a. India
    b. Australia
    c. West Indies
    d. England

25. Who was the first woman to score a century in both ODI and T20I formats?

    a. Smriti Mandhana
    b. Suzie Bates
    c. Tammy Beaumont
    d. Alyssa Healy

Quiz Answers

1. **A – Belinda Clark.** Belinda Clark was the first woman to score a double century in a One Day International, achieving this milestone in 1997.
2. **B – England.** England won the first ICC Women's World Cup in 1973, which was also the first global tournament for women's cricket, held before the men's World Cup began including women's teams.
3. **A – Jhulan Goswami.** Jhulan Goswami is the highest wicket-taker in Women's One Day Internationals, leading the list with her exceptional bowling performances.
4. **D – 2022.** Women's cricket made its debut at the Commonwealth Games in 2022, marking a significant milestone in the sport's inclusion in major multi-sport events.
5. **A – Rachael Heyhoe Flint.** Rachael Heyhoe Flint was the first woman to be inducted into the ICC Cricket Hall of Fame, recognizing her pivotal role in the development of women's cricket.
6. **A – First woman to score 7,000 runs.** Mithali Raj achieved the milestone of being the first woman to score 7,000 runs in Women's One Day Internationals, cementing her legacy as one of the greatest female cricketers.
7. **C – Anisa Mohammed.** Anisa Mohammed holds the record for the best bowling figures in a Women's T20 International, showcasing her skill as a leading spinner in women's cricket.
8. **A – Australia.** Australia has won the most ICC Women's World Cup titles, demonstrating their long-standing dominance in women's international cricket.
9. **A – First woman to play in a men's county cricket match.** Sarah Taylor broke significant barriers in English domestic cricket by becoming the first woman to play in a men's county cricket match.
10. **B – 2015.** The Women's Big Bash League (WBBL) was first introduced in 2015, enhancing the profile and competitive opportunities in women's cricket in Australia.

11. **A – Deandra Dottin.** Deandra Dottin was the first woman to score a century in a Women's T20 International, achieving this feat during the 2010 ICC Women's World Twenty20.
12. **A – Ellyse Perry.** Ellyse Perry has won the ICC Women's Cricketer of the Year award the most times, highlighting her all-round excellence in international cricket.
13. **B – 2016.** The first Women's Cricket Super League in England was held in 2016, designed to boost the professional level of women's cricket in the country.
14. **A – Jhulan Goswami.** Jhulan Goswami was the first woman cricketer to take 200 wickets in ODIs, marking a significant achievement in her illustrious career.
15. **C – Ellyse Perry.** Ellyse Perry was named Wisden Leading Woman Cricketer in the World in 2017, recognized for her outstanding performances across formats.
16. **C – 232.** The highest team score in Women's T20 internationals is 232, set by New Zealand against South Africa in 2018.
17. **C – Stafanie Taylorj.** Stafanie Taylor became captain of the West Indies women's cricket team in 2011 at the age of 21, making her one of the youngest players to assume national team leadership in women's cricket.
18. **B – Claire Polosak.** Claire Polosak has umpired in the most international cricket matches among women, making significant contributions to the sport.
19. **A – Highest individual score (232)*.** Amelia Kerr set the record for the highest individual score in a Women's ODI with 232* against Ireland in 2018.
20. **A – Isa Guha.** Isa Guha was the first female commentator in men's Test cricket, breaking new ground in cricket broadcasting.
21. **A – 2014.** The ICC introduced a Women's Championship in 2014 to determine qualification for the Women's World Cup, aiming to improve competitive balance and development.
22. **D – Julia Price.** Julia Price broke new ground by becoming the first woman to coach in a professional men's cricket league when she joined the coaching staff of the Brisbane Heat in the Big Bash League.

23. **A – 2004.** The first Women's Asia Cup was held in 2004, promoting women's cricket among Asian countries and enhancing regional competition.
24. **C – West Indies.** The West Indies hosted the first standalone ICC Women's T20 World Cup in 2018, marking a significant step in providing greater visibility and importance to women's cricket.
25. **B – Suzie Bates.** Suzie Bates was the first woman to score a century in both ODI and T20I formats, highlighting her prowess as a versatile and powerful batter.

Did You Know?

1. The first recorded women's cricket match dates back to 1745, played in Surrey, England, under the title "The Married vs The Unmarried."
2. Former England captain Charlotte Edwards became one of the first women to commentate during a men's England Test match in 2014.
3. The 2020 ICC Women's T20 World Cup final was the most-watched women's cricket match ever, drawing a global cumulative average audience of 89.2 million people.
4. In 2017, Clare Connor became the first woman appointed to the ICC's Cricket Committee.
5. In 2015, Kia became the first major sponsor for women's cricket in England, marking a significant development in commercial support for women's sports.
6. In 2019, Cricket Australia announced equal pay for women in their centrally contracted players, making it one of the first national sporting organizations to close the pay gap.
7. In 2017, the Women's Cricket World Cup Final at Lord's sold out, making it the first time the event had ever sold out, and was watched by millions worldwide.
8. Former England cricketer Ebony Rainford-Brent became the first black woman to commentate on English cricket, highlighting diversity advancements within sports media.

9. Women's cricket was among the first to trial new rules in T20 internationals, including allowing an extra fielder outside the inner circle in the last overs of the innings.
10. In 2018, the women's cricket team from India played their first-ever match at the iconic Lord's Cricket Ground, a landmark moment for women's cricket.
11. The ECB's "Chance to Shine" program has brought cricket to hundreds of thousands of girls in schools across the UK, aiming to foster a new generation of female cricketers.
12. The 2009 ICC Women's World Cup was pivotal in promoting women's cricket globally, being the first to be held alongside the men's tournament in Australia.
13. In 2020, Julia Price became the first female coach in the Big Bash League, serving as an assistant coach for the Brisbane Heat men's team.
14. In 2005, Pakistan established their first women's cricket team, challenging social norms and promoting sports participation among women in South Asia.

CHAPTER 13:
CRICKET COACHING AND DEVELOPMENT

1. What is the highest coaching certification level offered by the International Cricket Council (ICC)?

   a. Level 1
   b. Level 2
   c. Level 3
   d. Level 4

2. Which country was the first to establish a formal coaching program for cricket?

   a. Australia
   b. England
   c. India
   d. South Africa

3. Who is known for pioneering modern cricket coaching techniques?

   a. Bob Woolmer
   b. Gary Kirsten
   c. Mickey Arthur
   d. Duncan Fletcher

4. What year did the ICC Cricket Academy open in Dubai?

   a. 2000
   b. 2004
   c. 2009
   d. 2012

5. Which coaching method focuses on enhancing players' decision-making skills on the field?
   a. Game Sense
   b. Shadow practice
   c. Scenario training
   d. Technical drills

6. Who was the first full-time coach appointed by the England Cricket Board?
   a. Mike Brearley
   b. David Lloyd
   c. Trevor Bayliss
   d. Andy Flower

7. What innovative technology is widely used in cricket coaching for technique analysis?
   a. Hawk-Eye
   b. Video analysis software
   c. Virtual reality systems
   d. Sensor-equipped bats

8. Which cricket team introduced a computer analyst to assist with coaching in the late 1990s?
   a. Australia
   b. West Indies
   c. India
   d. England

9. What is the primary focus of grassroots cricket development?
   a. Winning international tournaments
   b. Increasing participation
   c. Scouting professional players
   d. Promoting private leagues

10. Who was the first woman to coach a national men's cricket team?
    a. Lisa Keightley
    b. Julia Price

c. Charlotte Edwards
   d. Clare Connor

11. Which of the following is a common method for talent identification in cricket?
    a. Open trials
    b. Player auctions
    c. Statistical analysis
    d. Public voting

12. What does 'bio-mechanical analysis' help coaches understand?
    a. Players' mental strength
    b. Players' physical movements
    c. Players' tactical knowledge
    d. Players' game history

13. Which tool is used to measure a bowler's speed?
    a. Radar gun
    b. Speedometer
    c. Pedometer
    d. Accelerometer

14. Which year did the ECB launch a significant initiative to promote inclusivity and diversity in cricket coaching?
    a. 2010
    b. 2015
    c. 2018
    d. 2020

15. What aspect of coaching is primarily addressed by psychological conditioning?
    a. Physical fitness
    b. Technical skills
    c. Mental toughness
    d. Team strategies

16. How often does the World Cricket Coaching Conference take place?

a. Every year
b. Every two years
c. Every three years
d. Every five years

17. What role does biomechanics play in cricket coaching?
    a. Helps in designing team jerseys
    b. Assists in understanding player movements to prevent injuries
    c. Determines the best cricket bat design
    d. Measures the crowd's noise levels

18. Which academy is known globally for its advanced cricket coaching facilities?
    a. MRF Pace Foundation
    b. National Cricket Academy, India
    c. Lahore Qalandars High-Performance Center
    d. Bradman Cricket Academy

19. What unique approach does 'shadow practice' involve?
    a. Practicing without a ball
    b. Playing only in shaded areas
    c. Competing against a virtual opponent
    d. Night-time training sessions

20. Which famous coach wrote the book "The Art and Science of Cricket"?
    a. Shane Warne
    b. John Buchanan
    c. Bob Woolmer
    d. Greg Chappell

21. What is considered the most important skill for a cricket coach?
    a. Technical knowledge
    b. Communication skills
    c. Playing experience
    d. Analytical abilities

22. Which online tool has revolutionized remote cricket coaching?

    a. Skype
    b. Coach's Eye
    c. Zoom
    d. YouTube

23. What is the primary goal of junior cricket leagues?

    a. Entertainment
    b. Education
    c. Talent identification
    d. Fitness

24. What is a common injury that cricket coaches try to prevent through proper training?

    a. Tennis elbow
    b. Runner's knee
    c. Bowler's arm
    d. Stress fractures

25. Who is credited with bringing a scientific approach to cricket fitness and nutrition?

    a. Ricky Ponting
    b. Virat Kohli
    c. Ben Stokes
    d. Chris Gayle

Quiz Answers

1. **C – Level 3.** The highest coaching certification level offered by the International Cricket Council (ICC) is Level 3.
2. **B – England.** England was the first country to establish a formal coaching program for cricket.
3. **A – Bob Woolmer.** Bob Woolmer is known for pioneering modern cricket coaching techniques, significantly influencing how coaches use technology and sports science today.
4. **C – 2009.** The ICC Cricket Academy opened in Dubai in 2009, providing advanced training facilities and programs.
5. **A – Game Sense.** Game Sense is a coaching method that focuses on enhancing players' decision-making skills on the field.
6. **B – David Lloyd.** David Lloyd was the first full-time coach appointed by the England Cricket Board.
7. **B – Video analysis software.** Video analysis software is widely used in cricket coaching for technique analysis, allowing detailed breakdowns of players' actions.
8. **C – India.** India introduced a computer analyst to assist with coaching in the late 1990s, becoming one of the first teams to use data extensively to improve performance.
9. **B – Increasing participation.** The primary focus of grassroots cricket development is increasing participation to ensure the sport grows at the community level.
10. **B – Julia Price.** Julia Price was the first woman to coach a national men's cricket team, breaking significant gender barriers in the sport.
11. **A – Open trials.** Open trials are a common method for talent identification in cricket, giving players a platform to showcase their skills.
12. **B – Players' physical movements.** 'Bio-mechanical analysis' helps coaches understand players' physical movements, enhancing technique and preventing injuries.
13. **A – Radar gun.** A radar gun is used to measure a bowler's speed, providing immediate feedback on their delivery speed.
14. **C – 2018.** In 2018, the ECB launched the "South Asian Action Plan," a significant initiative aimed at increasing participation

and promoting inclusivity among diverse communities, aligning with broader efforts to develop cricket inclusively and sustainably in England and Wales.

15. **C – Mental toughness.** Psychological conditioning in coaching primarily addresses mental toughness, helping players cope with the pressures of competitive cricket.
16. **A – Every year.** The World Cricket Coaching Conference takes place every year, gathering coaching professionals from around the world to discuss advances and techniques.
17. **B – Assists in understanding player movements to prevent injuries.** Biomechanics plays a crucial role in cricket coaching by helping understand player movements to prevent injuries and improve performance.
18. **B – National Cricket Academy, India.** The National Cricket Academy in India is known globally for its advanced cricket coaching facilities.
19. **A – Practicing without a ball.** 'Shadow practice' involves practicing the movements of cricket without actually using a ball, helping players focus on their technique.
20. **C – Bob Woolmer.** Bob Woolmer wrote "The Art and Science of Cricket," combining his deep knowledge of the game with modern coaching techniques.
21. **B – Communication skills.** Communication skills are considered the most important for a cricket coach, enabling effective teaching and understanding with players.
22. **B – Coach's Eye.** Coach's Eye has revolutionized remote cricket coaching by allowing coaches and players to analyze techniques in detail through video analysis.
23. **C – Talent identification.** The primary goal of junior cricket leagues is talent identification, aiming to find and nurture future cricket stars.
24. **D – Stress fractures.** Stress fractures are a common injury that cricket coaches try to prevent through proper training, focusing on technique and physical conditioning.
25. **B – Virat Kohli.** Virat Kohli is credited with bringing a scientific approach to cricket fitness and nutrition, emphasizing the importance of physical conditioning in the modern game.

Did You Know?

1. The first cricket coaching manual was published in 1851 by John Nyren, offering a glimpse into the coaching techniques of the early 19th century.
2. In 2007, Shivani Mishra became one of the first female cricket coaches to lead a men's international cricket team, specifically Qatar's national team.
3. The ICC has conducted cricket coaching courses in over 50 different countries to help spread cricket knowledge and improve global competitiveness.
4. The 'Snickometer', part of cricket's technology coaching tools, was invented in the 1990s to detect faint edges from the bat, revolutionizing how coaches address players' batting techniques.
5. Cricket coaching camps have been set up in conflict zones such as Afghanistan to help young people find solace and structure through sports.
6. During the COVID-19 pandemic, many cricket boards, including Cricket Australia, started offering virtual coaching clinics to continue player development despite lockdowns.
7. The National Cricket Academy in India uses biomechanical analysis to fine-tune bowlers' actions to prevent injuries and improve performance.
8. In 2020, New Zealand Cricket introduced the world's first AI cricket coach, capable of providing players with detailed performance analysis.
9. Modern cricket coaching includes a significant focus on mental health, with teams employing sports psychologists to enhance mental toughness and concentration.
10. The ECB's 'South Asian Action Plan', launched in 2018, aims to attract more coaches from diverse backgrounds to reflect the multicultural love for cricket in England and Wales.
11. Countries like Australia and South Africa have established high-performance centers dedicated exclusively to refining elite cricket talent through advanced coaching methodologies.

12. Cricket coaching now often includes detailed nutritional plans tailored to individual players to optimize performance and recovery.
13. Some cricket academies teach environmental stewardship, promoting the use of sustainable materials and practices in sports.
14. Coaches at the international level sometimes receive cultural sensitivity training to better manage diverse teams, especially in countries with players from various backgrounds.
15. Specialized coaching courses are now available for coaching disabled cricket players, aiming to be inclusive and to promote the sport among all interested participants.

CHAPTER 14:
CRICKET IN POP CULTURE

1. Which famous novel features a crucial cricket match as part of the story?

    a. "Pride and Prejudice" by Jane Austen
    b. "Murder at the Vicarage" by Agatha Christie
    c. "A Passage to India" by E.M. Forster
    d. "Netherland" by Joseph O'Neill

2. What is the name of the Bollywood film where the protagonist is an aspiring cricketer?

    a. "Lagaan"
    b. "Chak De! India"
    c. "Kai Po Che!"
    d. "Iqbal"

3. Which song by 10cc features cricket sounds and a reference to the sport in its lyrics?

    a. "I'm Not in Love"
    b. "Dreadlock Holiday"
    c. "The Things We Do for Love"
    d. "Rubber Bullets"

4. Which documentary focuses on the West Indies cricket team's dominance in the 1970s and 1980s?

    a. "Fire in Babylon"
    b. "The Edge"
    c. "Death of a Gentleman"
    d. "Out of the Ashes"

5. Who is a famous musician known for his profound love of cricket, often seen at matches?

   a. Mick Jagger
   b. Elton John
   c. David Bowie
   d. Paul McCartney

6. Which comic book character is named after a cricket term?

   a. Silver Surfer
   b. The Joker
   c. Nightwing
   d. Batman

7. In which animated series does a character use cricket as a form of martial arts?

   a. "Samurai Jack"
   b. "Avatar: The Last Airbender"
   c. "The Simpsons"
   d. "Teen Titans"

8. What is the title of the cricket-themed episode in the British TV series "Downton Abbey"?

   a. "The Last Ball"
   b. "Cricket Fever"
   c. "A Game of Cricket"
   d. "The Match"

9. Which cricket player had a cameo in the Hollywood film "Pirates of the Caribbean"?

   a. Brian Lara
   b. Ian Botham
   c. Sir Viv Richards
   d. Shane Warne

10. What cricket-themed novel won the Booker Prize?

    a. "Selection Day" by Aravind Adiga
    b. "Netherland" by Joseph O'Neill

c. "Chinaman" by Shehan Karunatilaka
d. "The Art of Fielding" by Chad Harbach

11. Which television show featured a cricket match to resolve a dispute between characters?

    a. "Friends"
    b. "The Office"
    c. "The Crown"
    d. "Frasier"

12. Who is the author of "Beyond a Boundary", a book considered one of the greatest on cricket?

    a. CLR James
    b. Peter Roebuck
    c. Ed Smith
    d. Mike Atherton

13. Which rock band's music video shows the members playing cricket in the desert?

    a. The Rolling Stones
    b. Def Leppard
    c. Dire Straits
    d. Queen

14. What is the name of the fictional cricket team in the Indian TV series "Inside Edge"?

    a. Mumbai Mavericks
    b. Delhi Daredevils
    c. Chennai Super Kings
    d. Kolkata Knights

15. Which cricket term is commonly used in pop culture to denote a sudden, decisive victory?

    a. Duck
    b. Sweep
    c. Smash
    d. Bail out

16. What video game series is known for its detailed cricket simulation?

    a. Don Bradman Cricket
    b. Cricket 19
    c. Ashes Cricket
    d. All of the above

17. Who wrote "Playing It My Way", a biography that provides an inside look into a cricketer's life?

    a. Sachin Tendulkar
    b. Ricky Ponting
    c. Kevin Pietersen
    d. Virat Kohli

18. Which cricket player is known for their distinctively philosophical quotes, influencing many outside of sports?

    a. M.S. Dhoni
    b. Imran Khan
    c. Geoffrey Boycott
    d. Viv Richards

19. In which reality TV show did a former cricket star participate and gain significant public attention?

    a. Big Brother
    b. Survivor
    c. The Amazing Race
    d. Dancing with the Stars

20. What famous poet was known for his love of cricket, often writing about the sport in his poems?

    a. W.B. Yeats
    b. Sir John Betjeman
    c. Philip Larkin
    d. T.S. Eliot

21. Which famous cricketer had a brief music career, releasing a pop album in the 1980s?

a. Ian Botham
   b. Viv Richards
   c. Sunil Gavaskar
   d. Kapil Dev

22. What popular children's book features a cricket-playing character who teaches life lessons?

    a. "Charlotte's Web"
    b. "Harry Potter and the Philosopher's Stone"
    c. "James and the Giant Peach"
    d. "The Very Hungry Caterpillar"

23. Which horror film incorporates a cricket bat as a weapon?

    a. "Shaun of the Dead"
    b. "The Shining"
    c. "It"
    d. "Halloween"

24. Which poet famously described cricket in his work as "flannelled fools at the wicket"?

    a. Rudyard Kipling
    b. Francis Thompson
    c. G.K. Chesterton
    d. Robert Bridges

25. Which TV crime drama included a cricket scene that was key to solving the mystery of the episode?

    a. "Sherlock"
    b. "Agatha Christie's Poirot"
    c. "Midsomer Murders"
    d. "Law & Order"

Quiz Answers

1. **D - "Netherland" by Joseph O'Neill.** "Netherland" by Joseph O'Neill prominently features cricket as a central theme, exploring the protagonist's experiences in New York and using the sport as a metaphor for his feelings of alienation and quest for belonging.
2. **D - "Iqbal".** "Iqbal" is a Bollywood film where the protagonist, a young boy from a rural village in India, aspires to be a cricketer despite his deaf and mute condition.
3. **B - "Dreadlock Holiday".** The song by 10cc features cricket sounds and references to the sport in its lyrics.
4. **A - "Fire in Babylon".** This documentary focuses on the West Indies cricket team's dominance during the 1970s and 1980s.
5. **A - Mick Jagger.** The famous musician is known for his profound love of cricket, often seen at matches.
6. **D - Batman.** This comic book character is named after a cricket term.
7. **B - "Avatar: The Last Airbender".** In this animated series, a character uses cricket as a form of martial arts.
8. **C - "A Game of Cricket".** This is the title of the cricket-themed episode in the British TV series "Downton Abbey."
9. **C - Sir Viv Richards.** This cricket player had a cameo in the Hollywood film "Pirates of the Caribbean."
10. **C - "Chinaman" by Shehan Karunatilaka.** "Chinaman" by Shehan Karunatilaka, which explores the life of a washed-up journalist and a mysterious cricketer, won the Commonwealth Book Prize and the DSC Prize for South Asian Literature, but it did not win the Booker Prize.
11. **D - "Frasier".** In the television show "Frasier," there is an episode in which a cricket match is played to settle a dispute. The episode titled "Love Thy Neighbor" from Season 4 features the characters engaging in a cricket match, which is used as a comedic element to advance the plot and resolve conflicts among the characters.
12. **A - CLR James.** CLR James is the author of "Beyond a Boundary," considered one of the greatest books on cricket.

13. **C – Dire Straits.** The rock band's music video shows the members playing cricket in the desert.
14. **A – Mumbai Mavericks.** This is the name of the fictional cricket team in the Indian TV series "Inside Edge."
15. **B – Sweep.** This cricket term is commonly used in pop culture to denote a sudden, decisive victory.
16. **D – All of the above.** Don Bradman Cricket, Cricket 19, and Ashes Cricket are all video game series known for their detailed cricket simulation.
17. **A – Sachin Tendulkar.** Sachin Tendulkar wrote "Playing It My Way," a biography that provides an inside look into a cricketer's life.
18. **B – Imran Khan.** This cricket player is known for their distinctively philosophical quotes, influencing many outside of sports.
19. **D – Dancing with the Stars.** Former cricket stars like Darren Gough and Mark Ramprakash have participated in "Dancing with the Stars" in various countries, gaining significant public attention through their performances on this popular dance competition show.
20. **B – Sir John Betjeman.** This famous poet was known for his love of cricket, often writing about the sport in his poems.
21. **C – Sunil Gavaskar.** This famous cricketer had a brief music career, releasing a pop album in the 1980s.
22. **C – "James and the Giant Peach".** This popular children's book features a cricket-playing character who teaches life lessons.
23. **A – "Shaun of the Dead".** This horror film incorporates a cricket bat as a weapon.
24. **C – G.K. Chesterton.** This poet famously described cricket in his work as "flannelled fools at the wicket."
25. **C – "Midsomer Murders".** This TV crime drama included a cricket scene that was key to solving the mystery of the episode.

Did You Know?

1. Cricket has been featured in several literary classics, including Charles Dickens' "The Pickwick Papers," where Mr. Pickwick observes a game of cricket.
2. Many cricketers have made appearances in films and television shows. Sir Ian Botham, for instance, appeared in an episode of the British detective drama "Inspector Morse."
3. The sport has been referenced by many poets, including Harold Pinter, who famously wrote about the game's rhythms and pauses, reflecting deeper themes of time and memory.
4. The iconic music video for "Sledgehammer" by Peter Gabriel features animated cricket bats, subtly nodding to Gabriel's love for the sport.
5. Cricket has been humorously depicted in numerous animated series, including "Tom and Jerry," where Tom attempts to play the game only to be thwarted by Jerry.
6. The band Duckworth Lewis Method, named after the famous cricket scoring system, dedicates all its songs to cricket, blending pop music with cricket commentary and lore.
7. Celebrities such as Daniel Radcliffe and Hugh Grant are known cricket enthusiasts, often spotted at cricket grounds during significant matches.
8. The "Bowled Over" art exhibition, held in London, showcased cricket-themed artworks by various artists, illustrating the game's cultural impact beyond sports.
9. In an unusual fusion of cricket and ballet, the English National Ballet performed a piece inspired by cricket's movements and historical ties to dance, choreographed by Ruth Brill.
10. High fashion has also drawn inspiration from cricket, with designers like Ralph Lauren and Alexander McQueen incorporating cricket sweaters and whites into their collections.
11. Popular board games like Monopoly have featured special editions that include famous cricket venues such as Lord's as properties to buy and sell.

12. Cricket imagery is frequently used in advertisements to evoke themes of teamwork and fair play, especially in countries where the sport is a significant part of the culture.
13. There have been theatre productions solely dedicated to exploring cricket's history and its impact on society, blending drama with live cricket action on stage.
14. Large-scale murals depicting famous cricketers can be found in cities like Mumbai and Melbourne, celebrating the sport's heroes in vibrant, public artworks.
15. Around the world, there are several cricket-themed restaurants where diners can enjoy memorabilia-filled spaces and watch live games, fully immersing in the cricket culture.

CHAPTER 15:

FUTURE OF CRICKET IN THE UK

1. What is the ECB's primary initiative to increase cricket participation among children in the UK?
    a. Chance to Shine
    b. All Stars Cricket
    c. Cricket Unleashed
    d. Dynamos Cricket

2. Which city in the UK is set to have a new state-of-the-art cricket stadium by 2025?
    a. London
    b. Manchester
    c. Birmingham
    d. Bristol

3. What is the focus of the ECB's "Inspiring Generations" strategy?
    a. Enhancing player salaries
    b. Expanding women's cricket
    c. Building more cricket grounds
    d. Growing the game from grassroots to elite levels

4. Which technology is predicted to become more prevalent in UK cricket broadcasts by 2030?
    a. Virtual reality replays
    b. Drone camera coverage
    c. 4D broadcasting
    d. AI commentators

5. By what year does the ECB aim to achieve full professionalization of women's county cricket?

    a. 2025
    b. 2030
    c. 2035
    d. 2040

6. What innovative format is being promoted by the ECB to attract a younger audience?

    a. The Hundred
    b. T10 leagues
    c. Indoor cricket leagues
    d. 3D cricket

7. Which UK city is pioneering eco-friendly cricket grounds?

    a. Edinburgh
    b. Cardiff
    c. Leeds
    d. Liverpool

8. What major change is proposed in the governance of cricket clubs in the UK?

    a. Implementing salary caps
    b. Increasing diversity quotas
    c. Mandating environmental sustainability
    d. Requiring youth development programs

9. What is the projected increase in cricket viewership in the UK due to streaming platforms by 2030?

    a. 10%
    b. 25%
    c. 50%
    d. 75%

10. Which is the next big city expected to host an international ICC event in the UK?

    a. Nottingham
    b. Sheffield

c. Newcastle
   d. Glasgow

11. What initiative is being considered to combat pace of play concerns in cricket?

    a. Shorter formats
    b. Strict time penalties
    c. More powerplays
    d. Automated umpiring

12. How is artificial intelligence expected to aid in cricket coaching in the UK?

    a. Player selection
    b. Technique correction
    c. Game strategy development
    d. All of the above

13. What is the expected role of biomechanics in future UK cricket training?

    a. Injury prevention
    b. Performance enhancement
    c. Equipment design
    d. Player rehabilitation

14. Which UK university is leading research in cricket analytics?

    a. Oxford University
    b. Cambridge University
    c. Loughborough University
    d. Imperial College London

15. What is being done to improve the inclusivity of cricket in the UK?

    a. Multilingual coaching
    b. More urban cricket facilities
    c. Increased investment in women's cricket
    d. All of the above

16. What future innovation is considered for cricket equipment?

a. Smart cricket balls
b. Lighter, more durable bats
c. Customizable pads
d. Environmentally friendly gear

17. How is climate change expected to impact cricket seasons in the UK?

    a. Longer seasons
    b. Shorter seasons
    c. More indoor games
    d. No impact anticipated

18. What new fan engagement strategy is the ECB considering?

    a. Augmented reality apps
    b. Interactive fan zones at grounds
    c. Loyalty programs
    d. Virtual meet-and-greets with players

19. Which is seen as a future challenge for cricket clubs in the UK?

    a. Funding
    b. Player recruitment
    c. Spectator interest
    d. Media rights negotiations

20. What role will sports psychology play in the future of UK cricket?

    a. Enhancing team dynamics
    b. Individual mental training
    c. Crisis management
    d. All of the above

21. What is the predicted trend for cricket tourism in the UK?

    a. Increase due to global events
    b. Decrease due to virtual reality experiences
    c. Stabilization with traditional tourism
    d. Shift towards eco-tourism

22. What new rule is being considered to speed up the game?

a. Less time for innings breaks
b. Penalties for slow over rates
c. Reduced time for DRS decisions
d. Shorter powerplays

23. How are future cricket training facilities expected to evolve?

   a. Integration with other sports
   b. Specialized for weather conditions
   c. Use of robotic trainers
   d. All of the above

24. What demographic shift is expected to influence cricket in the UK?

   a. Aging population
   b. Increasing diversity
   c. Youth disinterest
   d. Urban migration

25. What is a major goal for sustainability in cricket by 2030?

   a. Zero waste matches
   b. Fully solar-powered stadiums
   c. Carbon-neutral tournaments
   d. Water recycling systems in grounds

Quiz Answers

1. **B – All Stars Cricket.** The ECB's primary initiative to increase cricket participation among children in the UK.
2. **C – Birmingham.** Birmingham is set to have a new state-of-the-art cricket stadium by 2025.
3. **D – Growing the game from grassroots to elite levels.** The focus of the ECB's "Inspiring Generations" strategy is to grow the game comprehensively.
4. **A – Virtual reality replays.** Virtual reality replays are predicted to become more prevalent in UK cricket broadcasts by 2030.
5. **A – 2025.** The ECB aims to achieve full professionalization of women's county cricket by 2025.
6. **A – The Hundred.** The innovative format being promoted by the ECB to attract a younger audience is The Hundred.
7. **B – Cardiff.** Cardiff is pioneering eco-friendly cricket grounds in the UK.
8. **B – Increasing diversity quotas.** A major change proposed in the governance of cricket clubs in the UK is increasing diversity quotas.
9. **C – 50%.** The projected increase in cricket viewership in the UK due to streaming platforms by 2030 is 50%.
10. **D – Glasgow.** Glasgow is the next big city expected to host an international ICC event in the UK.
11. **B – Strict time penalties.** An initiative being considered to combat pace of play concerns in cricket is the implementation of strict time penalties.
12. **D – All of the above.** Artificial intelligence is expected to aid in cricket coaching in the UK in player selection, technique correction, and game strategy development.
13. **D – Player rehabilitation.** Biomechanics significantly contributes to player rehabilitation in cricket, using detailed analyses of athletes' movements to design individualized recovery programs and prevent future injuries by correcting biomechanical faults. This application helps ensure players can return to their sport efficiently and safely, reducing the risk of re-injury.

14. **C – Loughborough University.** Loughborough University is leading research in cricket analytics in the UK.
15. **D – All of the above.** Improving the inclusivity of cricket in the UK involves multilingual coaching, more urban cricket facilities, and increased investment in women's cricket.
16. **A – Smart cricket balls.** A future innovation considered for cricket equipment is smart cricket balls.
17. **C – More indoor games.** Climate change is expected to result in more indoor games for cricket in the UK due to increased rainfall and unpredictable weather patterns, making outdoor play more challenging. This shift aims to ensure that matches can still proceed despite adverse weather conditions, thus adapting the sport to changing climate conditions.
18. **A – Augmented reality apps.** The ECB is considering augmented reality apps as a new fan engagement strategy.
19. **A – Funding.** Funding is identified as a future challenge for cricket clubs in the UK, as securing financial resources is crucial for maintaining operations, developing facilities, and supporting player development.
20. **A – Increase due to global events.** The predicted trend for cricket tourism in the UK is an increase due to global events.
21. **B – Penalties for slow over rates.** A new rule being considered to speed up the game involves penalties for slow over rates.
22. **D – All of the above.** Future cricket training facilities are expected to evolve with integration with other sports, specialization for weather conditions, and the use of robotic trainers.
23. **B – Increasing diversity.** The demographic shift expected to influence cricket in the UK is increasing diversity.
24. **C – Carbon-neutral tournaments.** A major goal for sustainability in cricket by 2030 is hosting carbon-neutral tournaments.
25. **C. Carbon-neutral tournaments.** A major goal for sustainability in cricket by 2030 is to achieve carbon-neutral tournaments. This involves reducing the carbon footprint associated with cricket events and offsetting any remaining emissions to reach net zero.

Did You Know?

1. By 2030, the ECB plans to make all cricket stadiums in the UK fully sustainable, using solar panels and rainwater harvesting systems to reduce environmental impacts.
2. The ECB is developing virtual reality cricket simulations to be introduced in schools, aiming to engage the younger generation in cricket through technology.
3. As part of an urban initiative, pop-up cricket pitches are expected to appear in city centers across the UK to promote the sport in densely populated areas.
4. The ECB is exploring the use of AI to predict player injuries and performance patterns, potentially revolutionizing how teams are managed and games are played.
5. Future plans include mandatory mental health training and support for all players in county and national teams, emphasizing the importance of mental well-being.
6. The ECB aims to double the number of female participants by 2025, making significant investments in facilities and coaching for women's cricket.
7. Innovative cooling technologies are being developed to keep pitches playable during increasingly hot summers, ensuring that cricket can continue despite rising temperatures.
8. In an effort to reach a global audience, the ECB is planning to offer match broadcasts in multiple languages, including virtual reality options for an immersive viewing experience.
9. Trials are underway for a new 'smart cricket ball' that can provide real-time data on spin, speed, and seam position, which could be used in live broadcasts and coaching.
10. Celebrity cricket leagues are in planning stages, aimed at increasing the sport's popularity by involving high-profile figures from other entertainment industries.
11. The ECB is introducing initiatives to make cricket more accessible to people with disabilities, including adaptive equipment and specialized coaching techniques.

12. Considering the UK's often unpredictable weather, more floodlit facilities are being built to allow cricket to be played during the evening, increasing participation rates.
13. Future marketing campaigns by the ECB will involve players as ambassadors in non-sporting fields such as fashion and music, broadening cricket's appeal.
14. The ECB plans to host annual international coaching conferences in London, aiming to make the city a global hub for cricket coaching excellence.
15. Future cricket stadiums in the UK are being designed with retractable roofs and movable seating to accommodate multiple sports and community events, maximizing their use.

CONCLUSION

As we draw the covers on this comprehensive exploration of cricket, it is clear that the sport is much more than just a game. It is a rich tapestry woven from history, culture, innovation, and human spirit. Through the quizzes, answers, and enlightening "Did You Know?" sections in this book, we've journeyed through the illustrious past, vibrant present, and the promising future of cricket, uncovering the depth and diversity that the sport embodies.

Each chapter aimed to not only test your knowledge but to expand it, offering insights into the significant events, legendary figures, and groundbreaking advancements that have defined cricket over the years. Trivia encapsulated in these pages highlights the universality of cricket and its unique ability to inspire, unite, and entertain people around the globe.

We hope that this book has deepened your appreciation for cricket and perhaps even introduced you to aspects of the game you were previously unaware of. Whether you've used this book to sharpen your cricket trivia prowess, to enhance your understanding of the game, or simply as a leisurely read, we trust that it has been as enjoyable to explore as it was for us to compile.

Cricket's journey continues, and with every match, player, and innovation, new stories and records will emerge to challenge and charm the next generation of fans. Keep watching, playing, and enjoying cricket, for the beauty of this game lies in its perpetual ability to surprise and captivate.

Printed in Dunstable, United Kingdom